Renewable Energy for Beginners

A Student's Guide to Clean Energy and Green Careers

BY

Sam O. Alamu

Copyright © 2025 Sam O. Alamu.

All rights reserved.

No part of this book may be reproduced, stored in a retrieval system, or transmitted in any form or by any means—electronic, mechanical, photocopying, recording, or otherwise—without the prior written permission of the publisher, except in the case of brief quotations used in reviews or critical articles.

ISBN: 979-8-9906976-7-2 (E-book)
ISBN: 979-8-9906976-8-3 (paperback)
ISBN: 979-8-9906976-9-0 (hardcover)

Library of Congress Cataloging-in-Publication Data

Names: Alamu, Samuel O., author.

Title: Renewable energy for beginners: a student's guide to clean energy and green careers

Library of Congress Control Number: 2025947358

Identifiers: LCCN 2025947358 (print)

LC record available at https://lccn.loc.gov/2025947358

Published by Author Vicinity
[Alpharetta, Georgia, United States]

Cover design by Author Vicinity
Illustrations by Author Vicinity

Printed in the United States of America
First Edition: 2025

Dedication

To my son, Josh, whose early steps symbolize a future worth striving for and whose presence inspires ongoing commitment to the triple nexus of energy, education, and environment.

To my wife, Maggie, whose intelligence, resilience, and steadfast support have been instrumental in my personal and professional growth.

To emerging scholars and advocates in sustainability: May this work contribute to your journey.

And to all students I have mentored—from primary education to advanced research—your pursuit of knowledge fuels my dedication to teaching and discovery.

Foreword

Our world stands at a critical juncture, where bold transitions in how we produce and use energy are no longer optional but essential. Building a sustainable energy future depends not only on innovation and policy but also on equipping the next generation with the knowledge and motivation to lead change. This book, "Renewable Energy for Beginners – A Student's Guide to Clean Energy and Green Careers" serves this mission with clarity and purpose.

It introduces students to the fundamentals of renewable energy and its real-world applications, while also providing valuable insight into the diverse and growing landscape of green careers. Its content is both accessible and technically sound, presented in a way that informs, inspires, and challenges young minds to think critically about the world's energy needs.

As a professor of sustainable energy systems and a long-time researcher in geothermal, biomass, and renewable energy technologies, I recognize the urgent need for more materials like this—resources that demystify energy concepts for younger generations around the world, including those in underrepresented and underserved communities. Dr. Alamu has succeeded in making this complex topic engaging, relevant, and approachable.

I have known the author, Dr. Sam O. Alamu, for several years through his doctoral research and academic collaboration. During his visit to my research group at Cornell University, he demonstrated not only strong technical knowledge but also a deep commitment to clean energy education and inclusive innovation. His dedication to creating accessible learning tools for young people, particularly those often left out of technical conversations, is commendable and needed.

With more than four decades in sustainable energy research and education, I can attest to the importance of resources like this. With over 300 scientific publications and multiple co-authored books in the field, I am continually reminded that the next wave of innovation starts with curiosity sparked early. This book offers that spark. It introduces key principles of energy generation, distribution, sustainability, and equity in a way that is both informative and inspiring. I highly recommend it to students, educators, and anyone seeking a strong foundation in renewable energy and pathways to careers that make a difference.

This guide is timely, thoughtfully written, and rooted in both academic integrity and a sincere desire to inspire. I commend Dr. Alamu for this important contribution to energy education and encourage educators, parents, and institutions to use it as a tool to build awareness, interest, and capacity for the future leaders in our global clean energy transition.

— Dr. Jefferson W. Tester

Croll Energy Fellow, Atkinson Center for a Sustainable Future

Principal Scientist, Cornell Earth Source Heat Project
Professor of Sustainable Energy Systems
Smith School of Chemical and Biomolecular Engineering, Cornell University
Fellow, Royal Society of Chemistry

Acknowledgments

First and foremost, I give all glory to God, who has brought me this far as a first-generation scholar. This journey has been one of grace, growth, and unwavering faith, and I am deeply grateful for the wisdom, strength, and direction He continues to provide me with from elementary education till now.

To my parents, who planted seeds of discipline and perseverance, and to my siblings, who have cheered me on through every stage of my academic and professional journey, thank you for your love and unwavering support.

I am especially thankful for the countless students I have had the honor to teach across all levels of education in different countries of the world. Your curiosity and hunger for knowledge are the heartbeat of this book.

I would like to express my gratitude to Professor Jefferson W. Tester for his thoughtful mentorship throughout my academic journey and for graciously contributing the foreword to this book, lending his voice as a distinguished expert in the field of sustainable energy.

To my colleagues and mentors in academia and the energy industry, your insights, collaborations, and encouragement helped shape the technical depth and practical vision behind this work. I'm particularly grateful to the institutions that continue to support clean energy education and innovation, and to those who are working tirelessly to empower future leaders in sustainability.

Finally, to my dear family and friends, thank you for your sacrifices, faith, and unwavering encouragement. To my wife, Maggie, and our son, Josh—your love and presence have been both my anchor and my inspiration throughout this journey. This work stands as a reflection of our shared hope and commitment to a cleaner, brighter future.

May this book educate, inspire, and empower a new generation to become bold stewards of the planet and champions of sustainable progress.

Table of Contents

Dedication III

Foreword.. IV

Acknowledgments VI

Preface 2

Chapter 1   Introduction To Renewable Energy 4

Chapter 2   The Importance Of Renewable Energy 8

Chapter 3   Different Kinds Of Renewable Energy.. 16

Chapter 4   Solar Energy 23

Chapter 5   Wind Energy 34

Chapter 6   Hydropower Energy 42

Chapter 7   Tidal Energy 49

Chapter 8   Biomass Energy 59

Chapter 9   Geothermal Energy... 75

Chapter 10   From Power Plant To Plug — How Electricity Gets To You 79

Chapter 11   Energy Storage Solutions 83

Chapter 12   The Future Of Renewable Energy 92

Chapter 13   Professional Career In Renewable Energy And How To Get Involved 100

Chapter 14   Essential Equations For Renewable Energy Calculations 108

Chapter 15   Resources And Further Reading..112

Glossary 116

Preface

Welcome to the transformative world of renewable energy! This book is your guide to understanding the powerful role of clean, sustainable energy sources in shaping our future. Whether you are a curious student, an aspiring scientist, or someone passionate about making a positive impact, this book will provide you with the knowledge and inspiration needed to embark on an exciting journey toward a career in renewable energy.

As the renowned environmentalist Lester R. Brown once said, "The great transition from fossil fuels to renewable sources of energy is underway." This shift is not only crucial for addressing climate change but also for building a sustainable and resilient future for all. Renewable energy technologies such as solar, wind, and geothermal power offer solutions that are both innovative and practical, helping to mitigate the environmental impacts of traditional energy sources while fostering economic growth and job creation.

In alignment with the United Nations Sustainable Development Goals (SDGs), particularly Goal 7: Affordable and Clean Energy, this book explores how renewable energy can be harnessed to provide clean, reliable, and affordable power for everyone.

"Renewable energy is the peace plan of the 21st century."

–António Guterres,
the UN Secretary-General

By investing in renewable energy, we are not only ensuring a healthier planet but also promoting peace and stability through sustainable development.

Throughout this book, you will discover the fascinating technologies that make renewable energy possible. From the photovoltaic cells in solar panels to the blades of wind turbines, we will delve into the science and engineering behind these innovations. You will learn about real-world applications, such as how solar power is used in schools, businesses, and farms to reduce energy costs and carbon footprints. Also highlighted in this book are the latest advancements in the field, including energy storage solutions and smart grid technologies, which are revolutionizing how we generate and use energy.

This book is more than just a collection of facts and figures. It is a call to action. As future leaders and change-makers, you have the opportunity to be at the forefront of the renewable energy revolution. I encourage you to participate in hands-on projects, join renewable energy clubs, and explore career pathways in this dynamic and growing industry. According to the International Renewable Energy Agency (IRENA), the renewable energy sector could employ over 42 million people globally by 2050. This means that your passion and skills can directly contribute to building a sustainable future.

Knowledge is power. Through this book, I aim to empower you to make smart, informed choices about how we use and conserve energy. Each chapter is designed to be engaging and accessible, filled with colorful illustrations, real-life examples, and inspiring stories from experts and pioneers in the field.

As the environmental advocate Vandana Shiva reminds us, "The future of humanity and of our planet lies in our hands." It is up to us to shape it, and renewable energy is a key part of this transformation.

Together, we can create a world where renewable energy powers our lives, and sustainability is at the heart of everything we do. Thank you for joining us on this journey. Let's explore the amazing world of renewable energy and discover how you can be a part of the change.

Chapter 1

Introduction to Renewable Energy

What is Renewable Energy?

Renewable energy comes from natural sources that replenish themselves over short periods of time. Unlike fossil fuels, which take millions of years to form, renewable energy sources are constantly being renewed. Renewable energy helps reduce greenhouse gas emissions, decrease pollution, and mitigate the effects of climate change. It's also sustainable and can lead to energy independence.

Imagine waking up every day and having endless power from sources that never run out. That's what renewable energy is all about. Unlike fossil fuels like coal and oil, which take millions of years to form and can run out, renewable energy comes from natural resources that replenish themselves over short periods. These include sunlight, wind, rain, tides, waves, and geothermal heat. Figure 1.1 shows the example of renewable energy technology that was further discussed in this book.

Figure 1.1. Solar panels converting sunlight into electricity.

The Energy Story

Once upon a time, people relied on the sun, wind, and water for power. Ancient civilizations used wind to sail ships and the sun to grow crops. Fast forward to the Industrial Revolution, fossil fuels became the main energy source, powering factories, cars, and homes. However, burning fossil fuels creates pollution and contributes to climate change. Figure 1.2 illustrates the evolution of lighting technology, from early humans creating fire for heating millions of years ago, to the era of oil lamps, and finally to the modern use of solar lamps.

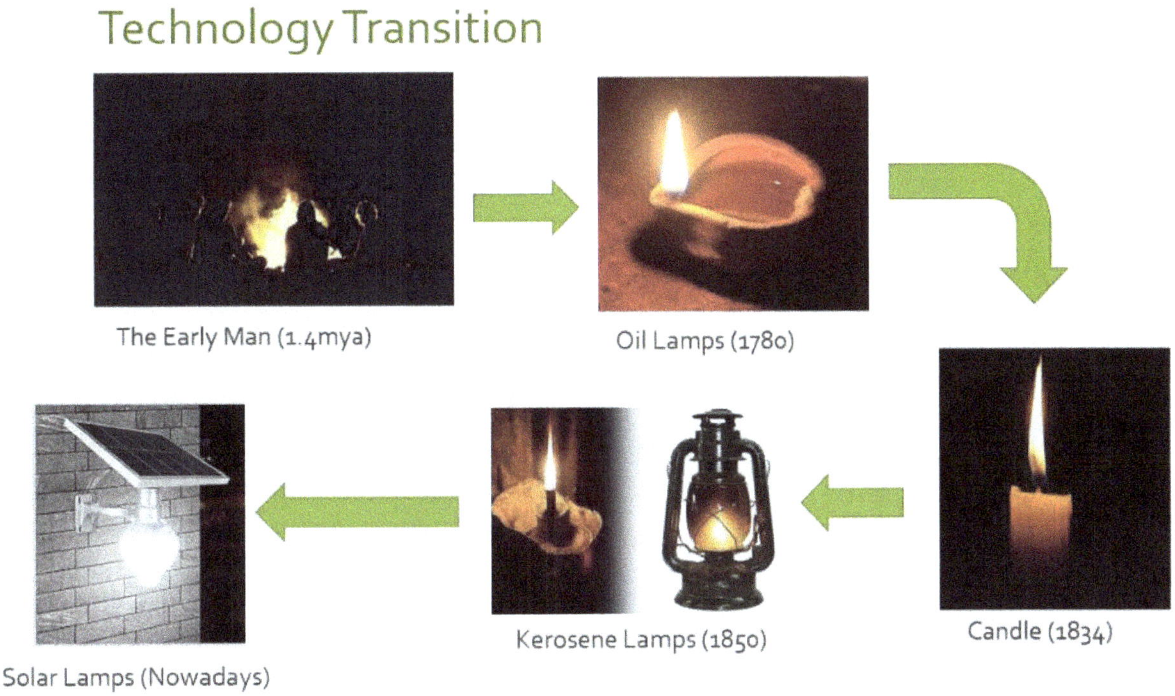

Figure 1.2. Evolution of lighting technology

The Renewable Energy Revolution

Now, we are amid a renewable energy revolution. Scientists and engineers are finding innovative ways to harness natural resources for clean, sustainable energy. Solar panels turn sunlight into electricity, wind turbines capture wind energy, and hydroelectric dams generate power from flowing water. These technologies help reduce pollution and provide a sustainable energy source for the future.

Why is Renewable Energy Important?

A. Protecting the Planet

Renewable energy is crucial for protecting our planet. Burning fossil fuels releases harmful pollutants into the air, contributing to global warming and climate change as shown in Figure 1.3 (a)—release of pollutant from diesel generator into air; (b) — indoor air pollution (a release of pollutant from domestic cooking using charcoal); (c)—release of air pollution from industrial stack pipe; and (d)—release of air pollution from transportation (cars, trucks, school buses etc.).

Figure 1.3. Sources of air pollutants

Renewable energy sources produce little to no emissions, helping to keep our air and water clean, protecting the environment and human health. Renewable energy reduces the reliance on fossil fuels, which are major sources of pollution and greenhouse gases.

B. Economic Benefits

Investing in renewable energy can boost the economy. It creates jobs in the manufacturing, installation, and maintenance of renewable energy systems. It also reduces energy costs in the long term and can make countries more energy independent.

C. Energy Security

Renewable energy enhances energy security by diversifying energy sources. Unlike fossil fuels, which are concentrated in certain parts of the world, renewable energy sources are available everywhere. This reduces dependence on imported fuels and increases resilience against energy supply disruptions.

Fun Fact

Did you know that the energy from the sun that reaches Earth in just one hour could meet the world's energy needs for an entire year? That's the power of renewable energy!

Renewable energy is the key to a sustainable and cleaner future. By harnessing the power of the sun, wind, water, and more, we can reduce pollution, create jobs, and protect our planet. As you continue reading, you will learn more about the exciting world of renewable energy and how you can be a part of this green revolution.

Chapter 2

The Importance of Renewable Energy

The Problem with Fossil Fuels

Fossil fuels like coal, oil, and natural gas have been the primary sources of energy for decades. However, burning these fuels releases harmful pollutants, including carbon dioxide (CO_2), into the atmosphere. This contributes to air pollution and climate change, leading to extreme weather conditions, melting ice caps, and rising sea levels.

Figure 2.1. Pollution caused by burning fossil fuels.

Sustainability: The Long-Term Solution

As the world faces serious environmental problems—like air pollution, climate change, and the overuse of natural resources, there is one idea that helps guide the solution and that is sustainability.

What is Sustainability?

Sustainability means meeting the needs of the present without compromising the ability of future generations to meet their own needs (United Nations, 1987). In other words, we should use natural resources wisely, protect the environment, and create systems that can last a long time—economically, socially, and ecologically (EPA, 2022). This idea was first widely defined in the 1987 Brundtland Report by the United Nations and has since become a guiding principle in everything from environmental protection to energy use and economic development.

In simple terms, sustainability is about living and making choices that protect our planet's resources, so that life on Earth can continue to thrive today, tomorrow, and long into the future.

The Three Pillars of Sustainability

Sustainability is built on three key pillars:

Environmental Sustainability: Protecting natural ecosystems, reducing pollution, and conserving resources like water, air, and forests.

Economic Sustainability: Building economies that provide jobs and wealth without relying on practices that harm the environment or cause long-term damage.

Social Sustainability: Ensuring everyone has access to basic needs like clean energy, education, healthcare, and opportunities—regardless of where they live or their background.

Figure 2.2. Three pillars of sustainability (Gevme, 2023)

These pillars work together. For example, when a community installs solar panels (environmental), it often creates local jobs (economic) and improves energy access for families (social). So, sustainable development requires balancing the three pillars as represented in Figure 2.2.

How Renewable Energy Supports Sustainability

Traditional energy sources like coal, oil, and gas release greenhouse gases that contribute to climate change. These fuels also take millions of years to form, which means they are non-renewable.

Renewable energy—such as solar, wind, hydropower, biomass, and geothermal—is different. These sources are naturally replenished, produce far less pollution, and help fight climate change (IEA, 2023).

Using renewable energy is one of the most powerful ways we can:

- Reduce greenhouse gas emissions
- Protect natural ecosystems
- Create long-term green jobs
- Build fair and healthy communities
- Preserve resources for future generations

That's why sustainability is at the heart of renewable energy. Clean energy technologies don't just solve today's problems, they help us build a better, more livable world for tomorrow.

Tied to Global Goals

Renewable energy and sustainability are major parts of the United Nations Sustainable Development Goals (SDGs)—specifically **Goal 7:** Affordable and Clean Energy and **Goal 13:** Climate Action. These goals are part of a worldwide effort to reduce poverty, protect the planet, and promote peace.

"Sustainability is no longer about doing less harm. It's about doing more good."

—Jochen Zeitz, sustainable business leader

The Renewable Energy Solution

Renewable energy sources, such as solar, wind, and hydropower, produce little to no emissions. By switching to renewables, we can significantly reduce air and water pollution, slow down global warming, and protect our planet for future generations. An example is shown in Figure 2.3, which illustrates a clean energy wind farm generating electricity without any pollution.

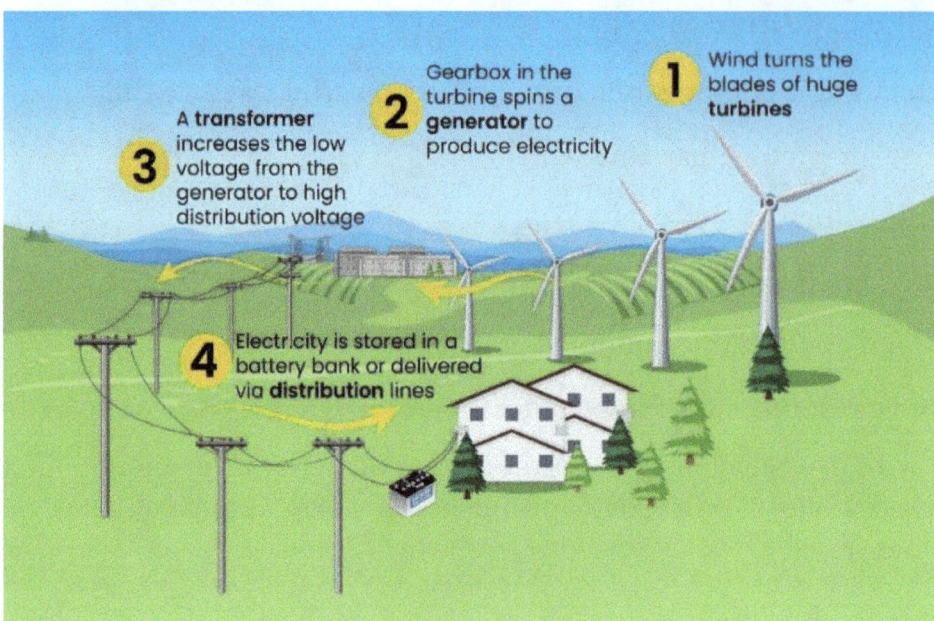

Figure 2.3. A clean energy wind farm generating electricity without pollution.

Economic Benefits Creating Jobs

The renewable energy sector is a major job creator. Jobs in this field range from manufacturing and installing solar panels and wind turbines to researching new technologies and maintaining existing systems. As the demand for renewable energy grows, so does the need for skilled workers.

Figure 2.4. Workers installing solar panels, creating new job opportunities.

Saving Money

While the initial cost of renewable energy systems can be high, they often save money in the long run. For example, solar panels can reduce electricity bills, and wind power can provide a stable, low-cost energy source for communities.

Case Study: Solar Savings

Imagine a high school installing solar panels on its roof. Initially, the school might spend a significant amount on installation. However, over the next 20 years, the school could save thousands of dollars on energy bills. These savings could be used to buy new computers, books, or sports equipment.

Figure 2.5. A school saving money with rooftop solar panels.

Energy Security

Diverse Energy Sources

Relying on a variety of renewable energy sources as shown in Figure 2.6 makes a country less dependent on imported fuels. This enhances energy security by ensuring a stable and continuous energy supply, even if there are disruptions in one part of the energy market.

Figure 2.6. Energy independence through diverse renewable energy sources.

Local Energy Production

Renewable energy can be produced locally, reducing the need for long-distance transportation of fuels. This local production not only boosts the local economy but also reduces the risks associated with fuel transportation, such as spills and accidents.

Fun Fact

Did you know that the largest wind turbines in the world –Haliade-X and MySE 16 stand 260 meters and 264 meters tall respectively? That's taller than the Statue of Liberty as shown in Figure 2.7. This gigantic turbine can generate enough electricity to power thousands of homes.

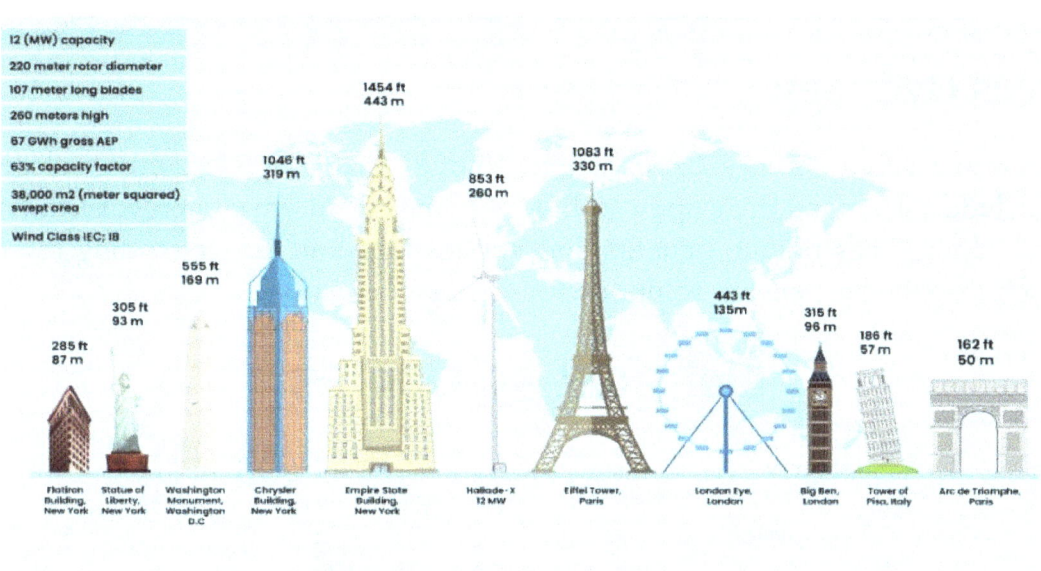

Figure 2.7. The largest wind turbine in the world.

Haliade-X manufactured by GE Wind Energy, was deployed as a prototype in 2019 with a 12 MW capacity but has been updated to 13 MW in year 2020 and commercially deployed in August 2023 with a generating capacity of 13 MW, having a total height of 260 meters (853 feet). The highest Haliade-X capacity of 14.7 MW is still a prototype, not commercially available. Currently, the largest operational wind turbine in the world, as of now, is the MySE 16–260 manufactured by Mingyang Smart Energy in China. It has a power output of 16 MW and a rotor diameter of 264 meters (866 feet).

Renewable energy is crucial for a sustainable future. It helps protect our environment, boosts the economy, and enhances energy security. By understanding the importance of renewable energy, we can all contribute to a cleaner, healthier planet.

Chapter 3

Different Kinds of Renewable Energy

Sources Overview

Renewable energy comes from natural sources that are constantly replenished. These include solar, wind, hydropower, biomass, and geothermal energy. Each type of renewable energy has unique benefits and applications and understanding these can help us choose the best energy solutions for different situations.

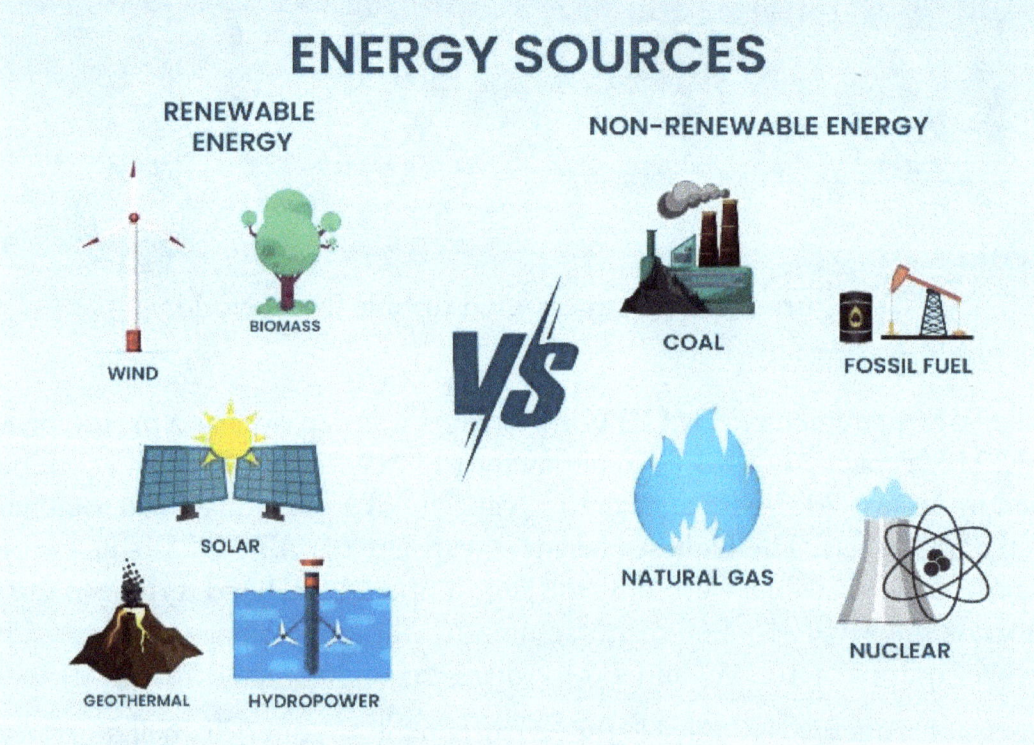

Figure 3.1. Renewable and non-renewable energy sources.

Pros and Cons of All Types of Renewable Energy

Solar Energy

Pros:

- **Abundant and Renewable**: The sun provides a nearly limitless supply of energy.

- **Low Operating Costs**: Once installed, solar panels have minimal maintenance and operational costs.
- **Environmental Benefits**: Solar energy produces no greenhouse gases during operation.
- **Scalability**: Solar systems can be installed at any scale, from small residential setups to large solar farms.

Cons:

- **Intermittent Energy Source:** Solar power generation is dependent on weather conditions and time of day.
- **High Initial Costs:** Installation of solar panels can be expensive, although costs are decreasing.
- **Space Requirements:** Large solar farms require significant land area.
- **Energy Storage Needs:** Effective energy storage solutions are necessary to manage supply during non-sunny periods.

Wind Energy

Pros:

- **Clean and Renewable**: Wind energy is a sustainable source with minimal **environmental impact.**
- **Low Operational Costs:** Wind turbines have relatively low maintenance costs once installed.
- **Scalability:** Wind farms can be built onshore and offshore, providing flexibility in location.
- **Job Creation:** The wind industry generates jobs in manufacturing, installation, and maintenance.

Cons:

- **Intermittent Supply:** Wind energy depends on wind availability, which can be inconsistent.
- **Noise and Aesthetic Issues:** Wind turbines can generate noise and are sometimes considered visually unappealing.

- **Wildlife Impact:** Wind turbines can pose a threat to birds and bats.
- **High Initial Costs:** The installation of wind turbines requires significant investment.

Hydropower

Pros:

- **Reliable and Consistent:** Hydropower provides a stable and continuous source of energy.
- **Low Operating Costs:** Hydropower plants have low maintenance and operational costs once built.
- **Energy Storage:** Hydropower plants can store energy by controlling water flow, providing flexibility in electricity supply.
- **Flood Control and Water Supply:** Dams can help manage water resources and prevent flooding.

Cons:

- **Environmental Impact:** Dams can disrupt local ecosystems and affect fish populations.
- **High Initial Costs:** Building dams and reservoirs requires substantial investment.
- **Displacement Issues:** Large hydropower projects can displace communities and wildlife.
- **Limited Suitable Locations:** Not all geographic locations are suitable for hydropower plants.

Biomass Energy

Pros:

- **Carbon Neutral:** Biomass energy can be considered carbon neutral as it involves the use of organic materials that absorb CO_2 during their growth.
- **Waste Reduction:** Utilizes agricultural, forestry, and urban waste, reducing

landfill use.

- **Versatile Energy Production:** Biomass can produce electricity, heat, and biofuels.
- **Economic Benefits:** Supports agricultural and forestry industries.

Cons:

- **Air Pollution:** Biomass combustion can produce pollutants and greenhouse gases.
- **Land and Water Use:** Large-scale biomass production requires significant land and water resources.
- **Efficiency Issues:** Biomass energy production can be less efficient compared to other renewables.
- **Sustainable Supply:** Overharvesting of biomass resources can lead to environmental degradation.

Geothermal Energy

Pros:

- **Reliable and Stable:** Provides a consistent and stable energy supply.
- **Low Emissions:** Produces very low levels of greenhouse gases.
- **Small Footprint:** Requires less land compared to solar or wind farms.
- **High Efficiency:** Geothermal plants can achieve high efficiency levels in electricity generation.

Cons:

- **Geographic Limitations:** Effective geothermal energy production is limited to regions with suitable geological conditions.
- **High Initial Costs:** Drilling and establishing geothermal plants can be expensive.
- **Earthquake Risk:** Geothermal drilling can induce seismic activity in some areas.
- **Resource Depletion:** Overuse of geothermal resources can lead to depletion and reduced energy output.

Tidal and Wave Energy

Pros:

- **Predictable and Reliable:** Tidal and wave energy are highly predictable and consistent.
- **Low Visual Impact:** Most tidal and wave energy systems are located offshore and have minimal visual impact.
- **Environmental Benefits:** Produces no greenhouse gases during operation.
- **Renewable Resource:** Utilizes the natural movement of water, a renewable resource.

Cons:

- **High Initial Costs:** Installation of tidal and wave energy systems can be very expensive.
- **Environmental Concerns:** Can impact marine ecosystems and coastal environments.
- **Limited Suitable Locations:** Effective tidal and wave energy production is limited to specific coastal areas.
- **Maintenance Challenges:** Harsh marine environments can pose challenges for maintenance and operation.

A quick overview of the pros and cons of renewable and non-renewable energy is presented in Table 3.1.

Table 3.1 Comparison of Renewable and Non-Renewable Energy

Feature	Renewable Energy	Non-Renewable Energy
Source	Natural processes that replenish (sun, wind, hydro, biomass, geothermal)	Finite (Dwindling)—Earth-mined resources like coal, oil, natural gas, uranium
Sustainability	Highly sustainable and long-term	Unsustainable—resources will eventually run out

Feature	Renewable Energy	Non-Renewable Energy
Environmental Impact	Low emissions; cleaner air and water	High emissions; contributes to pollution and climate change.
Reliability	Variable—depends on weather or natural cycles.	Consistent and controllable output.
Infrastructure	Growing; requires modernization and smart grid integration	Well-established; compatible with most existing grid systems.
Health Impact	Fewer health risks due to lower pollution levels	Higher risks of respiratory and cardiovascular diseases
Upfront Cost	Often high (due to installation of solar panels, wind turbines, etc.)	Typically lower, especially for existing power plants.
Operating Cost	Low to very low (sunlight and wind are free resources)	Variable—ongoing fuel extraction and processing add cost
Energy Storage	Requires batteries or other storage technologies for consistency	Easier to store and transport (especially oil and gas)
Economic Impact	Creates green jobs; promotes local energy independence	Subject to global market volatility and geopolitical factors

Conclusion

Renewable energy sources offer a range of benefits, including environmental sustainability, low operating costs, and job creation. However, each type of renewable energy also has its own set of challenges, such as high initial costs, environmental impacts, and geographic limitations.

Balancing these pros and cons is essential for developing a sustainable and efficient energy strategy.

Chapter 4

Solar Energy

How Solar Energy Works

Solar energy is one of the most accessible and widely used forms of renewable energy. It harnesses sunlight and transforms it into electricity or heat using two main methods: photovoltaic (PV) cells and concentrated solar power (CSP). PV cells (typically made from silicon are arranged in solar panels) absorb photons from sunlight, freeing electrons to generate direct current (DC) electricity, which is then converted to alternating current (AC) by an inverter for household or commercial use. CSP systems use mirrors to concentrate sunlight onto a receiver, producing heat that powers turbines or can be stored. Typical residential setups include solar panels installed on rooftops, an inverter, optional battery storage, and grid connectivity as shown in Figure 4.1 (a & b). An array of PV modules, connected in series and parallel, can be installed in solar farms to supply electricity to consumers via the grid.

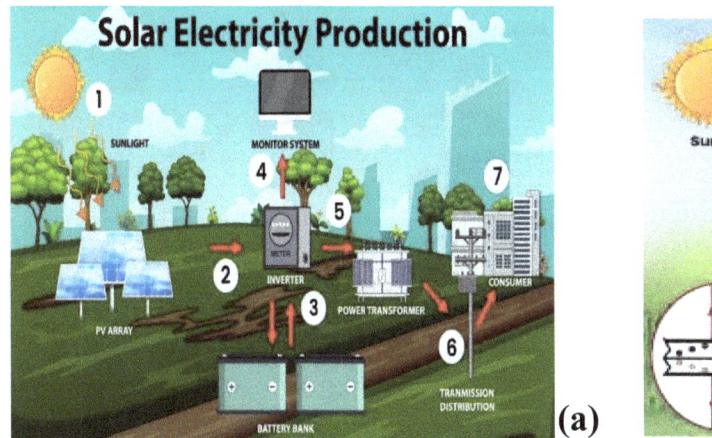 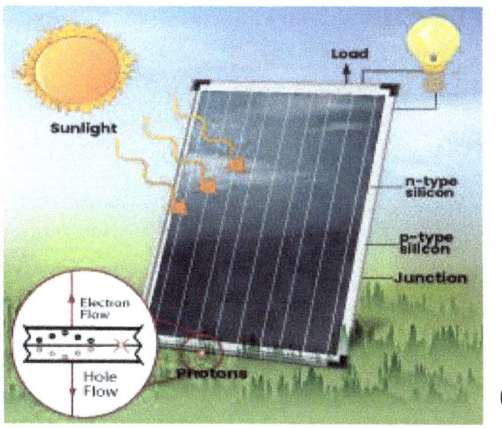

Figure 4.1 (a&b). Diagrams showing how solar panels convert sunlight into electricity.

Technological Advancements

A photovoltaic panel is a set of multiple photovoltaic (PV) cells connected in series or in parallel and positioned on the same support structure. The three main types of solar PV panels include: monocrystalline silicon PV panels, polycrystalline silicon PV panels, and thin-film PV panels (known as amorphous silicon).

Monocrystalline solar panels are the most efficient, with a conversion rate between 15% and 20%. To generate 1 kilowatt peak (kWp) of power, they require approximately 6m² of installation space. Polycrystalline photovoltaic panels offer lower efficiency (around 13% - 17%) than the monocrystalline ones and they need more area—around 8m² to produce 1 kWp. Thin-film panels, with an efficiency of about 6%, require the largest surface area, ranging from 11 - 13m² to achieve the same output.

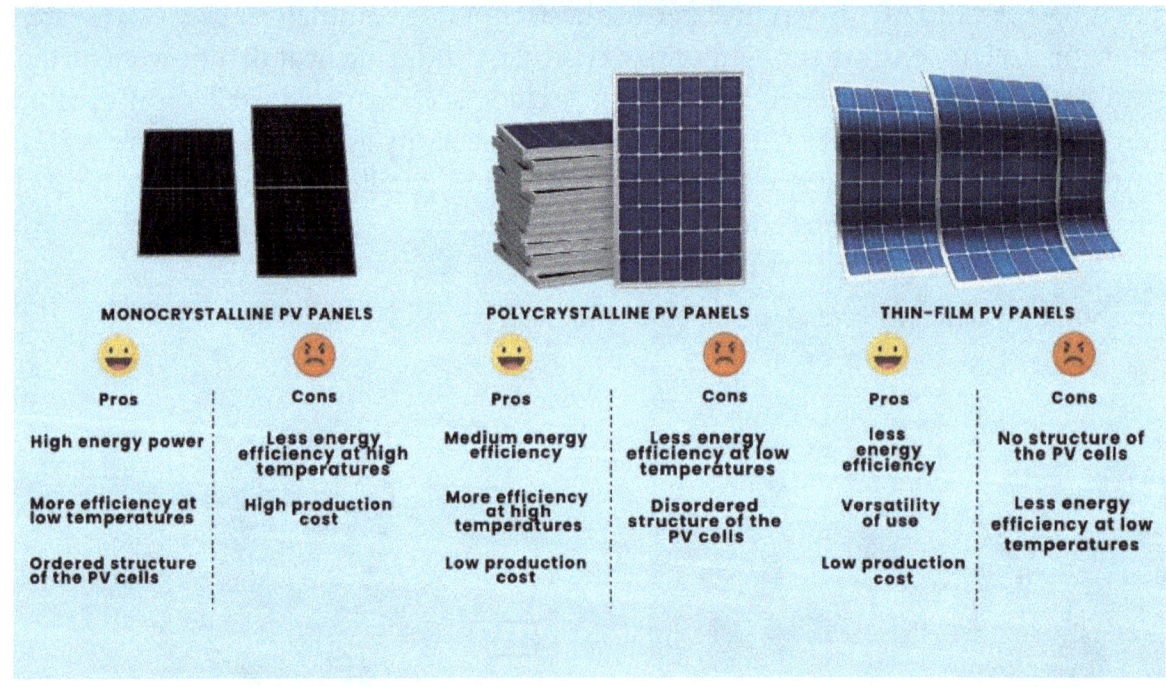

Figure 4.2. Types of solar PV panels

Improved Efficiency

Modern solar panels have seen significant improvements in efficiency. The average efficiency of commercial solar panels has increased from around 15% in the early 2000s to over 20% today. Cutting-edge research has led to the development of solar cells with efficiencies exceeding 25%. Figure 4.3 shows the increase in solar panel efficiency over the years.

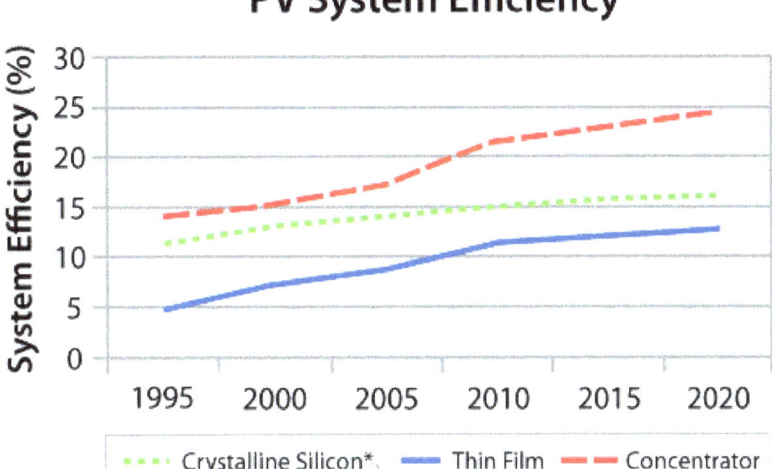

Figure 4.3. Efficiency of solar PV, then, now and future – solar photovoltaic (Han, 2014)

Bifacial Solar Panels

Bifacial solar panels are a recent innovation photovoltaic technology after innovation that can capture sunlight from both sides of the panel. A bifacial solar panel is a double-sided energy factory that transforms sunlight into electrical energy on both its top and bottom sides. This technology can increase energy production by up to 30% compared to traditional solar panels.

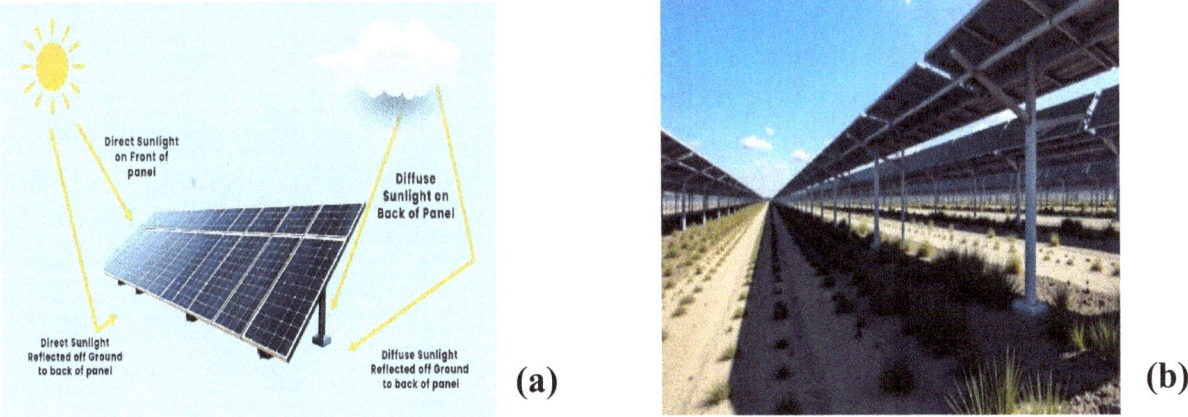

Figure 4.4 (a&b). Bifacial solar panels capturing sunlight from both sides.

Solar Tracking Systems

Solar tracking systems adjust the angle of solar panels throughout the day to follow the sun's path. This maximizes the amount of sunlight the panels receive and can increase energy production by 10-25%. A solar tracking system is composed of three well-differentiated components: the mechanism, the driving motors, and the tracking controller.

Applications of Solar Energy

Residential Use

Solar panels are commonly installed on the roofs of homes to provide electricity for household use. Homeowners can reduce their electricity bills and even earn money by selling excess power back to the grid.

Commercial and Industrial Use

Businesses and factories use large solar arrays to power their operations. Solar energy helps reduce operational costs and carbon footprints.

Solar Farms

Solar farms are large-scale installations that generate electricity for the grid. These farms can cover vast areas and produce significant amounts of renewable energy. A typical solar farm can contribute a substantial amount of power to the grid, depending on its size and location. For example, 1 MW solar farm can generate electricity for about 150-250 homes.

Figure 4.5. A large solar farm generating electricity for the grid.

The Solar Story: Solar in Schools

Let's imagine a school that installs solar panels on its roof. The panels generate enough electricity to power the school's lights, computers, and other electrical devices. The school saves money on energy bills, which it can then spend on new books, sports equipment, or other resources for students. This not only helps the school financially but also teaches students about the importance of renewable energy and sustainability.

Figure 4.6. Solar panels on school building rooftops.

As of 2024, over 8,000 K-12 schools in the United States use solar power, representing nearly 9% of all public and private schools. This number has grown significantly in recent years due to the increasing recognition of the cost savings and environmental benefits of solar energy.

According to a report from the U.S. Energy Foundation, the adoption of solar power in schools is driven by various factors, including the potential for substantial savings on energy costs, which are second only to teacher salaries in terms of school expenses. Schools often use power purchase agreements (PPAs) to install solar panels at little to no upfront cost, allowing them to purchase the generated electricity at a reduced rate over a set period.

Moreover, solar energy installations in schools also provide educational opportunities, giving students hands-on experience with renewable energy technology and preparing them for careers in the rapidly growing clean energy sector. For example, Denver Public Schools' Renewable Energy Academy trains high school students for jobs as solar installers, a field expected to expand significantly over the next decade. Additionally, many schools are pairing solar with battery storage to manage energy consumption and provide backup power, enhancing their resilience during power outages and emergencies.

Residential Solar Appliances

Common solar home appliances are shown in Figure 4.7.

The most common ones are as follows:

- **Solar Water Heaters**

Solar water heaters use sunlight to heat water for domestic use. They can significantly reduce energy bills and are relatively easy to install.

- **Solar-Powered Lights (Solar Lamps)**

Solar-powered lights are used for outdoor lighting, such as garden and pathway lights. They charge during the day and provide illumination at night.

- **Solar Chargers (Battery-pack)**

Solar chargers can charge small devices like smartphones and tablets. They are portable and useful for outdoor activities or emergency situations.

Figure 4.7. Solar home appliances

Commercial Solar Appliances

- ### Solar Panels for Businesses

Businesses install solar panels on rooftops or in parking lots to generate electricity, reducing energy costs and promoting sustainability.

- ### Solar-Powered HVAC Systems

Solar-powered HVAC (heating, ventilation, and air conditioning) systems use solar energy to provide climate control for buildings, improving energy efficiency.

Figure 4.8. HVAC systems that can be powered by solar energy.

- ## Solar-Powered Electric Vehicle (EV) Chargers

Businesses install solar-powered EV chargers to support electric vehicles. This helps reduce the carbon footprint of commuting and promotes green transportation.

Figure 4.9. Solar-powered EV chargers in a commercial setting.

Solar Appliances for Farms

- ## Solar-Powered Irrigation Systems

Solar-powered irrigation systems pump water for crops using solar energy. These systems are particularly useful in remote areas without access to the electrical grid.

Figure 4.10. Solar-powered irrigation system in use on a farm.

- ## Solar Electric Fences

Solar electric fences are used to contain livestock and protect crops from wildlife. They are powered by solar panels, making them reliable and cost-effective.

Figure 4.11. Solar-powered electric fence.

Renewable Energy for Beginners

- **Solar-Powered Farm Equipment**

Farm equipment like solar-powered tractors and grain dryers can significantly reduce fuel costs and emissions. These innovations help make farming more sustainable.

Figure 4.12. Solar-powered farm equipment.

Statistical Facts

- **Global Capacity**: As of 2022, the global installed capacity for solar energy is over 900 gigawatts, enough to power hundreds of millions of homes.

- **Cost Reduction**: The cost of solar power has dropped by more than 80% since 2010, making it one of the cheapest sources of electricity.

- **Job Creation**: The solar industry employs over 3 million people worldwide, from manufacturing to installation and maintenance.

Solar energy is a powerful tool in the fight against climate change. With advancements in technology, it is becoming more efficient and cost-effective. By harnessing the sun's energy, we can power our homes, businesses, and communities sustainably, ensuring a cleaner, greener future for all.

Conclusion

Solar appliances offer a wide range of benefits for homes, businesses, and farms. By utilizing solar energy, we can reduce energy costs, promote sustainability, and improve energy independence. As technology advances, more solar-powered devices will become available, making it easier to harness the power of the sun in our daily lives.

Chapter 5

Wind Energy

Wind energy is not just a local solution; it is a global phenomenon. Countries across the world are harnessing wind power to reduce greenhouse gas emissions, create jobs, and foster sustainable development.

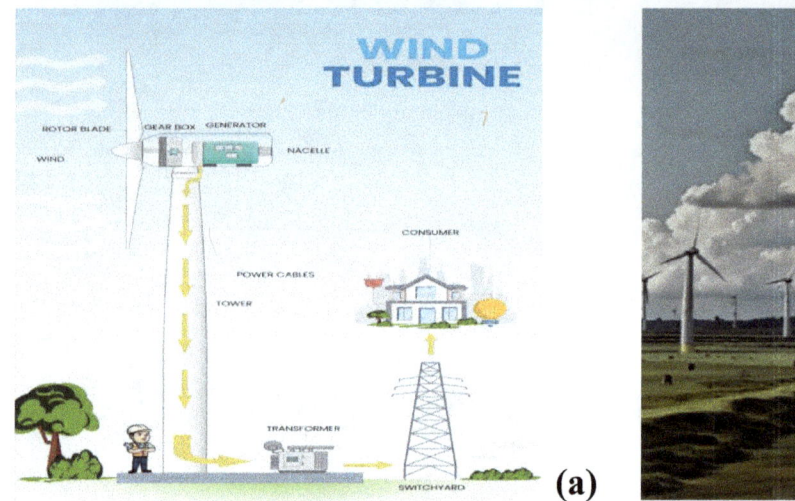 

(a) (b)

Figure 5.1 (a&b). Wind energy harnesses the power of the wind to generate electricity.

How Wind Energy Works

To generate electricity which is sent to the grid and finally to the consumer as shown in Figure 5.1. This process involves several key components and steps, from capturing wind with turbines to converting it into usable power.

Here's a breakdown of how it works:

Wind Turbines

Wind turbines are the primary devices used to convert wind energy in the form of kinetic energy to electrical energy. A typical wind turbine consists of the following parts:

- **Blades**: Modern wind turbines generally have three blades that capture the wind's kinetic energy.

- **Rotor:** The blades are attached to a hub, forming the rotor. When the wind blows, it causes the blades and rotor to spin.
- **Nacelle:** This is the housing on top of the tower that contains the generator, gearbox, controller, and other components.
- **Tower:** The tall structure that supports the rotor and nacelle, elevating them to a height where wind speeds are higher and more consistent.
- **Generator:** Converts the mechanical energy from the spinning rotor into electrical energy.

In summary, wind turbines use wind to generate electricity. As the wind blows, it turns the turbine blades, which spin a generator to produce electricity.

Capturing Wind Energy

- **Aerodynamics:** The blades are designed to be aerodynamic, which allows them to capture wind efficiently. As wind flows over the blades, it creates lift (similar to an airplane wing) and causes the rotor to spin.
- **Rotation:** The rotor's spinning motion turns a shaft connected to a generator inside the nacelle.

Generating Electricity

- **Generator:** The generator consists of magnets and coils of wire. When the rotor turns the shaft, it spins these components inside the generator, creating an electric current through electromagnetic induction.
- **Gearbox:** Some turbines use a gearbox to increase the rotational speed of the shaft before it reaches the generator, optimizing the generation of electricity.

Transmitting Electricity

- **Transformer:** The electricity generated is at a specific voltage that may need to be increased or decreased. A transformer adjusts the voltage to suitable levels for transmission.
- **Transmission Lines:** The electricity is then sent through transmission lines to a

substation, where it is distributed to homes, businesses, and other end users.

Integration with the Grid

Grid Connection: Wind turbines are connected to the electrical grid. Grid operators manage the distribution of electricity from wind farms along with other power sources to ensure a stable supply.

Wind Energy by Region

North America

North America, particularly the United States and Canada, has seen significant growth in wind energy capacity. The U.S. leads with substantial wind farms spread across states like Texas, Iowa, and Oklahoma. Texas alone generates more wind power than most countries, showcasing the region's potential. There are 239 wind-related projects in Texas and more than 15,300 wind turbines, the most of any state. Texas wind power generation surpassed the state's nuclear generation in 2014 and coal-fired generation in 2020.

Europe

Europe has been at the forefront of wind energy adoption, with countries like Germany, Denmark, and the United Kingdom leading the charge. Offshore wind farms are particularly prevalent in the North Sea, where strong winds provide a reliable source of energy.

Asia

China is the world leader in wind energy capacity, followed by India. These countries have invested heavily in wind power to meet their growing energy demands while reducing pollution. China's commitment to renewable energy is evident in its large-scale wind farms, both onshore and offshore.

Latin America

Latin America, particularly Brazil and Mexico, is rapidly expanding its wind energy sector. The region's favorable wind conditions and growing energy needs make it an ideal location for wind power projects.

Technological Advancements

Larger Turbines

The trend towards larger wind turbines continues, with modern turbines featuring longer blades and taller towers. These larger turbines capture more wind energy and operate more efficiently. The latest turbines can generate up to 15 MW of power, significantly more than earlier models.

Onshore wind farms are located on land, while offshore wind farms are built in shallow bodies of water, usually in the ocean. Both types of wind farms use wind turbines to generate electricity as a renewable energy source. Offshore wind farms are generally considered more efficient than onshore wind farms because of stronger, more consistent winds at sea. Offshore wind turbines can be much larger than onshore turbines, which can lead to greater economies of scale and more efficient energy generation. For example, the average onshore turbine is around 2.5–3 MW, while the average offshore turbine is 3.6 MW.

When wind turbines spin, they slow down the wind behind them and create swirling air called a "wake." This wake can make it harder for other turbines nearby to work well because the wind is weaker and more turbulent. To avoid this, wind farms space the turbines far enough apart so each one can catch stronger, cleaner wind. On land (onshore), the air mixes more quickly because of trees and hills, so turbines can be a bit closer together. But out at sea (offshore), the wind stays smooth and steady for longer, so turbines need to be spaced farther apart—usually about 7 to 9 times the width of their rotor blades. Proper spacing helps the whole wind farm produce more energy and keeps the turbines working safely and efficiently.

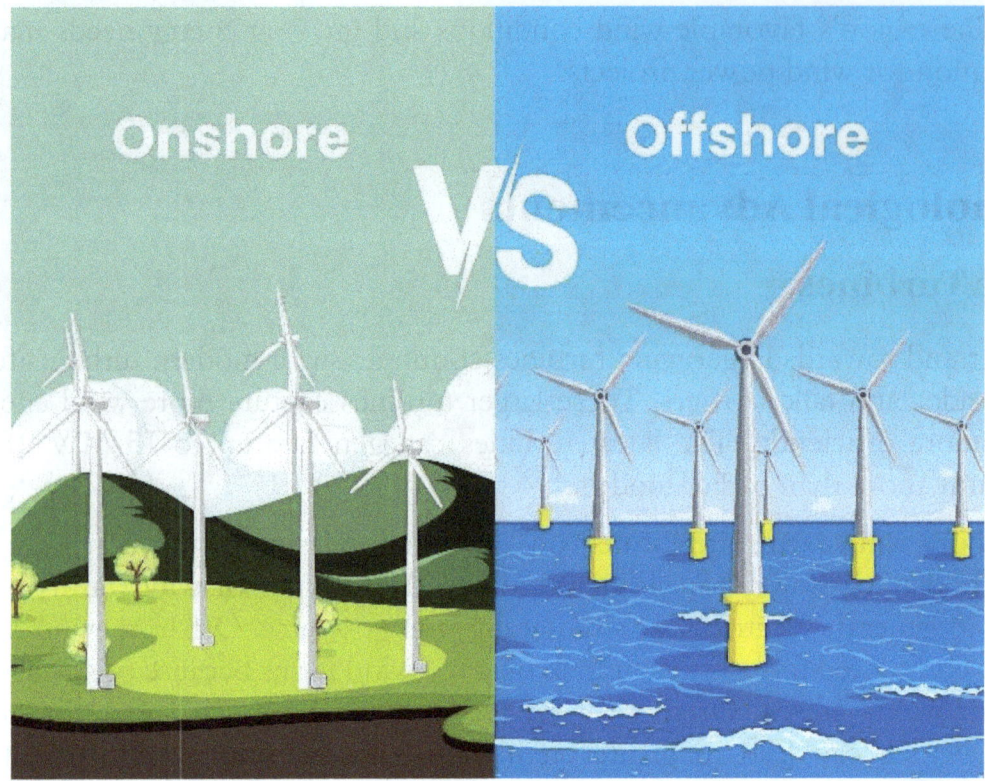

Figure 5.2. Onshore Vs offshore wind farm

Floating Wind Turbines

Floating wind turbines represent a major advancement, allowing for the installation of wind farms in deeper waters with depths of 50-1000 meters where winds are stronger and more consistent. These turbines are anchored to the seabed with mooring lines and can be deployed far offshore, reducing visual impact and competition for land use.

Figure 5.3. Floating wind turbine technology.

Digitalization and AI

The integration of digital technologies and artificial intelligence (AI) has revolutionized wind energy. Smart turbines equipped with sensors collect vast amounts of data, which AI analyzes to optimize performance and maintenance. Predictive maintenance reduces downtime and extends the lifespan of turbines.

Environmental and Economic Impacts

- **Clean Energy**: Wind energy produces no greenhouse gas emissions during operation, making it a key player in reducing carbon footprints.

- **Job Creation**: The wind energy sector creates numerous jobs in manufacturing, installation, maintenance, and research. As of 2020, the industry employed over 1.2 million people worldwide.

Real-Life Success Stories

The Danish Wind Energy Model

Denmark is a global leader in wind energy, generating nearly half of its electricity from wind power. The country's commitment to renewable energy began in the 1970s and has since grown into a robust industry. Denmark's success is attributed to strong government policies, public support, and continuous innovation.

Texas: The Wind Powerhouse

Texas, USA, is a prime example of how a region can harness its natural resources for wind energy. With vast open spaces and strong wind currents, Texas has become the leading state for wind power in the U.S., generating more than 30 GW of wind energy annually.

Statistical Facts

- **Global Capacity**: As of 2023, the global wind power capacity stands at over 800 GW, with China, the United States, and Germany leading in installations.
- **Cost Reduction**: The cost of wind energy has fallen by nearly 70% over the past decade, making it one of the most competitive sources of new power generation.
- **Job Creation**: The wind energy sector employs over 1.2 million people worldwide, with projections indicating this number could rise to 2 million by 2030.
- **Future Projections**: According to the International Energy Agency (IEA), wind energy could supply nearly 18% of global electricity by 2040, driven by technological advancements and supportive policies.

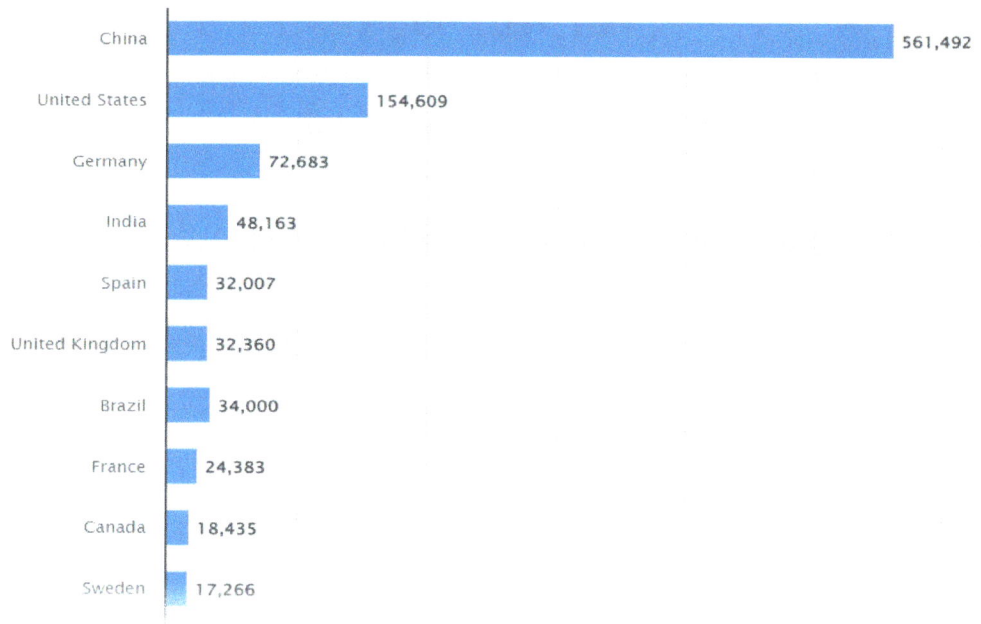

Figure 5.4. Cumulative installed capacity of wind power worldwide in 2024 in Megawatts (Statista, 2025)

Conclusion

Wind energy is a cornerstone of the global transition to renewable energy. Its rapid growth, driven by technological advancements and supportive policies, highlights its potential to significantly reduce greenhouse gas emissions and create economic opportunities. By understanding the global landscape of wind energy, you can appreciate the diverse and innovative ways different regions harness the power of the wind, contributing to a sustainable and resilient future.

Chapter 6

Hydropower Energy

Hydropower, also known as hydroelectric power, is one of the oldest and most reliable sources of renewable energy. It harnesses the energy of moving water to generate electricity and has been a cornerstone of renewable energy infrastructure worldwide.

Hydropower generates electricity by using the flow of water to drive turbines. This is often done in dams where water is stored and released as needed. Figure 6.1 shows the diagram of a typical hydropower plant showing the dam, reservoir, penstock, turbine, and generator.

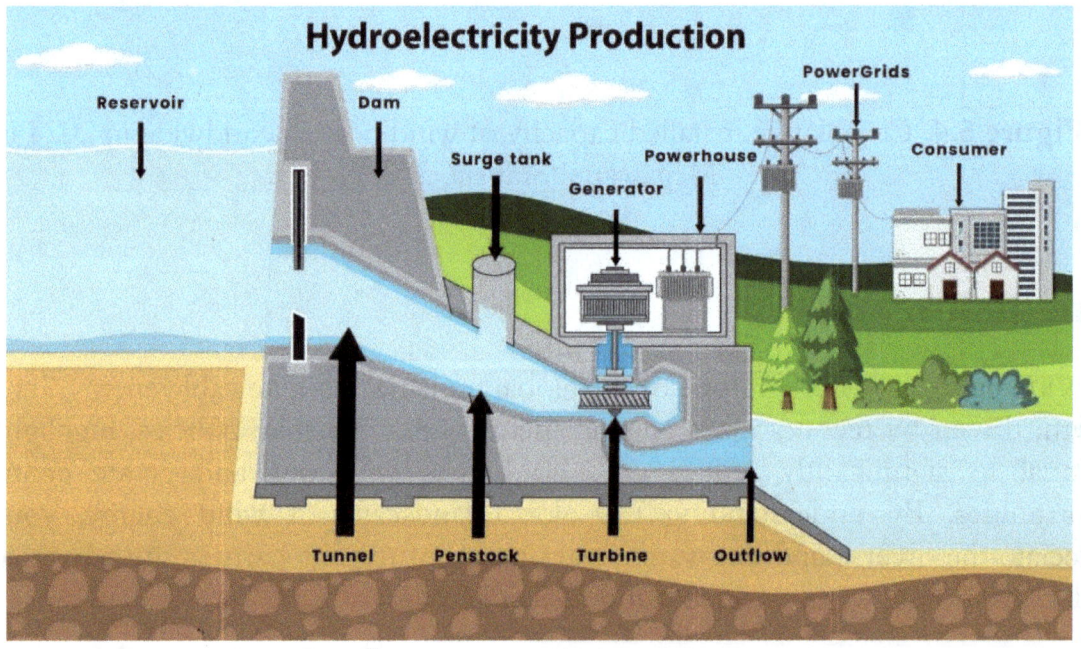

Figure 6.1. Hydropower plant generating electricity from flowing water.

How Hydropower Works

Hydropower generates electricity by using the flow of water to spin turbines connected to generators.

Hydropower systems convert the kinetic energy of flowing or falling water into mechanical energy, which is then transformed into electrical energy. The primary components of a hydropower system include:

- **Dam**: Creates a reservoir or diverts water to control the flow and generates a consistent water supply.

- **Reservoir**: Stores water that can be released as needed to generate power.

- **Penstock**: A large pipe that channels water from the reservoir to the turbines.

- **Turbines**: The water spins the turbines, converting kinetic energy into mechanical energy.

- **Generator**: Connected to the turbines, the generator converts mechanical energy into electrical energy.

- **Powerhouse**: Houses the turbines and generators.

Figure 6.2. Typical hydropower plant

Types of Hydropower Plants

1. **Run-of-the-River**: These plants do not require large reservoirs and rely on the natural flow of rivers. They are less invasive but can be less reliable during dry seasons.

2. **Reservoir (Conventional)**: These plants use dams to create large reservoirs,

allowing for the storage of water and a more consistent energy supply.

3. **Pumped Storage:** These plants pump water to a higher elevation during low demand and release it to generate electricity during high demand. Technological Advancements.

Fish-Friendly Turbines

Hydropower facilities currently provide 28.7% of all U.S. renewable energy and 6.2% of total U.S. electricity generation, but both the facilities and the environments they operate in are extremely diverse. As a result, there is no one-size-fits-all approach to fish passage.

One of the environmental concerns with traditional hydropower plants is their impact on aquatic life. Fish-friendly turbines are designed to reduce harm to fish passing through them, incorporating features like slower blade speeds and smoother surfaces. One example of an advanced turbine approach is Natel Energy's Restoration Hydro Turbine (RHT), a unique turbine design with thicker blades, rounded leading edges, and a forward slant to the blade that allows fish to safely move through hydropower facilities.

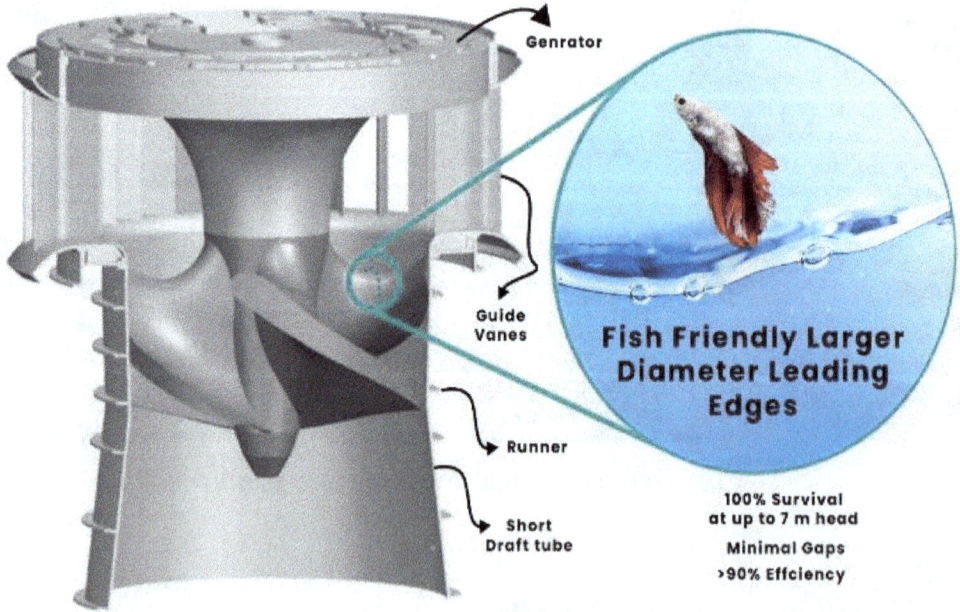

Figure 6.3. Fish-friendly turbine designed to minimize environmental impact.

Small-Scale Hydropower

Advancements in technology have led to the development of small-scale hydropower systems that can be installed in remote or off-grid locations. These systems provide a sustainable energy solution for communities without access to large-scale infrastructure.

Floating Solar-Hydro Integration

Combining floating solar panels with hydropower reservoirs is an emerging trend. This integration maximizes energy output by utilizing the same infrastructure for both solar and hydropower, enhancing efficiency and reliability.

Figure 6.4. Floating solar panels integrated with a hydropower reservoir.

Real-Life Success Stories

Three Gorges Dam, China

The Three Gorges Dam on the Yangtze River is the world's largest hydroelectric power station in terms of installed capacity (22,500 MW). It generates about 85 TWh (terawatt-hours) of electricity annually, providing power to millions of households and reducing China's reliance on coal. The dam is 7,660 feet long and 607 feet tall. When it was completed in 2006, it could produce enough electricity for 100 million people. In 2021, the dam generated 103.649 billion kWh.

Figure 6.5. The Three Gorges Dam, the largest hydroelectric power station in the world.

Itaipu Dam, Brazil-Paraguay

The Itaipu Dam, located on the Paraná River between Brazil and Paraguay, has a capacity of 14,000 MW and produces around 90 TWh of electricity annually. It supplies approximately 75% of Paraguay's electricity and 15% of Brazil's.

Figure 6.6. The Itaipu Dam, a major hydroelectric power source for Brazil and Paraguay.

Statistical Facts

- **Global Capacity**: As of 2023, the global hydropower capacity is over 1,300 GW, with China, Brazil, and the United States leading in installations.

- **Cost Efficiency**: Hydropower is one of the most cost-effective sources of renewable energy, with a low levelized cost of electricity (LCOE) compared to other sources.

- **Environmental Impact**: Hydropower plants reduce carbon emissions significantly. For example, the Itaipu Dam has avoided the emission of over 600 million tons of CO_2 since it began operating.

- **Job Creation:** The hydropower sector employs millions of people worldwide in construction, maintenance, and operation.

Conclusion

Hydropower is a cornerstone of renewable energy, offering a reliable and cost-effective source of clean power. With continuous technological advancements and growing global capacity, it plays a crucial role in the transition to a sustainable energy future. Understanding how hydropower works, its benefits, and its challenges can inspire the next generation to innovate and contribute to this vital field.

Chapter 7

Tidal Energy

Tidal energy harnesses the power of the ocean's tides to generate electricity, making it one of the most predictable and reliable forms of renewable energy. Unlike wind or solar power, which can be intermittent, tidal energy is driven by the gravitational forces between the Earth, moon, and sun, creating a steady and predictable flow of energy.

How Tidal Energy Works

Tidal energy is generated by capturing the kinetic and potential energy of moving water caused by the rise and fall of tides. The process involves using various technologies to convert this movement into electricity.

Tidal Barrages

A tidal barrage is a dam-like structure built across the entrance of a tidal basin or estuary. As the tide rises, water is trapped behind the barrage. When the tide drops, the stored water is released through turbines, generating electricity.

Example: The La Rance Tidal Power Station in France is one of the oldest and largest tidal power stations in the world, generating up to 240 MW of electricity.

Tidal Stream Generators

Tidal stream generators work similarly to underwater wind turbines. These devices are placed in fast-flowing tidal streams, where the movement of water turns the blades of the turbine, generating electricity.

Example: The MeyGen project in Scotland is one of the largest tidal stream energy projects, with an installed capacity of nearly 400 MW when fully operational.

Dynamic Tidal Power (DTP)

Dynamic Tidal Power is a more recent concept that involves constructing long dams extending from the coast into the sea. These dams are not designed to enclose a body of water like barrages but to create a pressure differential by harnessing the potential energy of tidal flows. This differential drives turbine located along the dam, generating electricity.

Example: Theoretical models suggest that DTP could be implemented on the coasts of China and South Korea, where tidal ranges are large, potentially generating gigawatts of power.

Tidal Lagoons

Tidal lagoons function similarly to tidal barrages but are designed as man-made structures that encircle a body of water. Water flows into the lagoon during high tide and is released through turbines during low tide.

Example: The proposed Swansea Bay Tidal Lagoon in Wales could generate around 320 MW of electricity, enough to power over 150,000 homes.

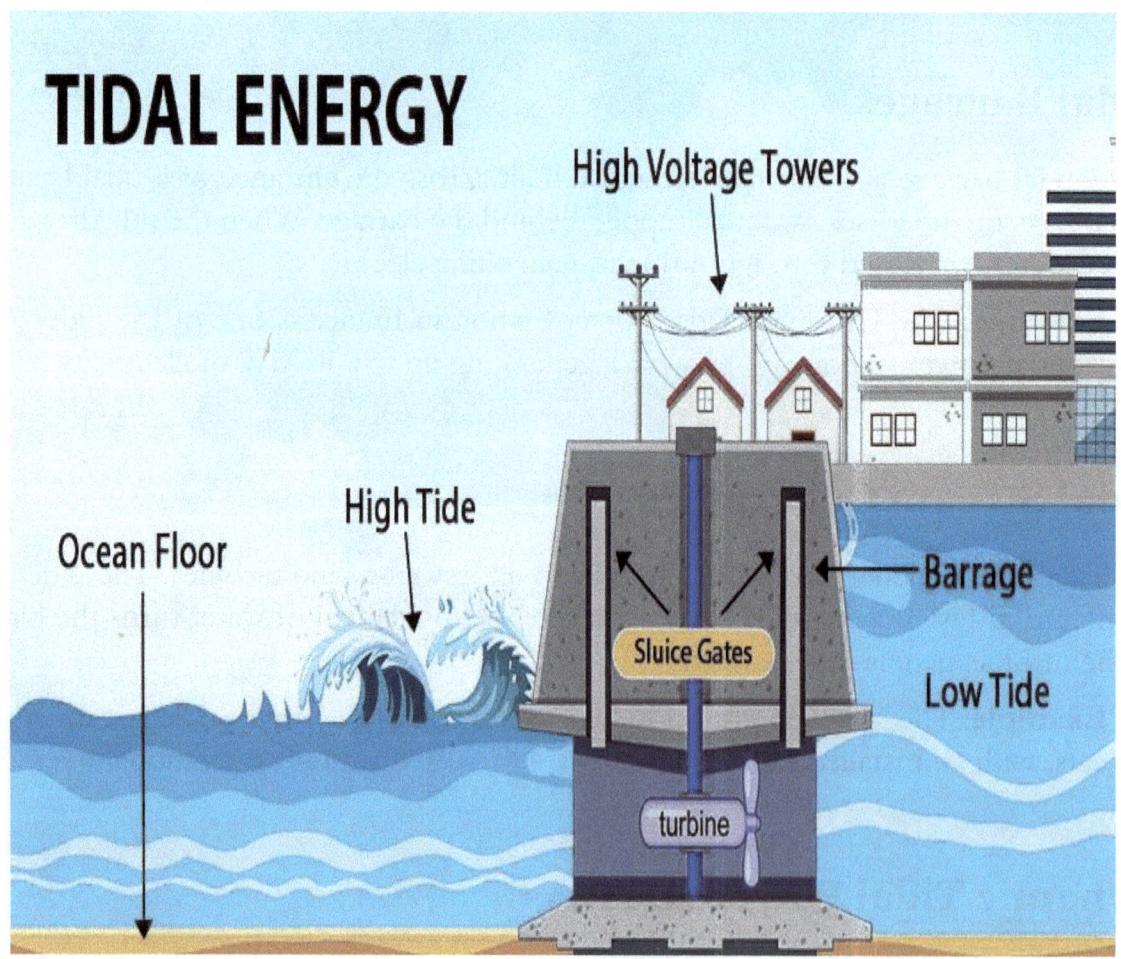

Figure 7.1. Diagram illustrating how tidal energy is generated.

Technological Advancements

Improved Turbine Designs

Recent advancements in turbine technology have led to the development of more efficient and durable tidal turbines. These turbines are designed to operate in harsh underwater environments, withstanding strong currents and corrosion.

Example: The AR1500 turbine, used in the MeyGen project, features a robust design that can operate at water speeds up to 5 meters per second, increasing energy capture efficiency.

Floating Tidal Platforms

Floating tidal platforms are a recent innovation that allows turbines to be anchored in deeper waters where tidal currents are stronger. These platforms adjust to changing water levels and can be deployed in a wider range of locations.

Example: Nova Innovation's Shetland Tidal Array uses floating platforms to harness the strong currents around the Shetland Islands, generating clean energy for local communities.

Hybrid Systems

Hybrid tidal systems combine tidal energy with other forms of renewable energy, such as wind or solar power. These systems can generate electricity even when tidal conditions are not ideal, ensuring a more consistent energy supply.

Example: The European Marine Energy Centre (EMEC) in Orkney, Scotland, is experimenting with hybrid systems that combine tidal and wave energy, maximizing energy production.

Figure 7.2. Advanced tidal turbine designs.

Real-Life Applications

South Korea's Sihwa Lake Tidal Power Station

The Sihwa Lake Tidal Power Station is the world's largest tidal power installation, with a capacity of 254 MW. It was built by converting a former estuary into a tidal basin. The station not only generates electricity but also helps improve water quality in the area.

Impact: The station produces enough energy to power over 500,000 homes annually, reducing reliance on fossil fuels and cutting carbon emissions.

Figure 7.3. Sihwa lake tidal power station, South Korea.

United Kingdom's MeyGen Project

The MeyGen project in Scotland is a leading example of tidal stream energy, with its turbines generating clean energy from the powerful currents in the Pentland Firth. The project has the potential to expand, eventually powering over 175,000 homes.

Impact: MeyGen demonstrates the commercial viability of tidal stream energy, contributing to the UK's renewable energy goals.

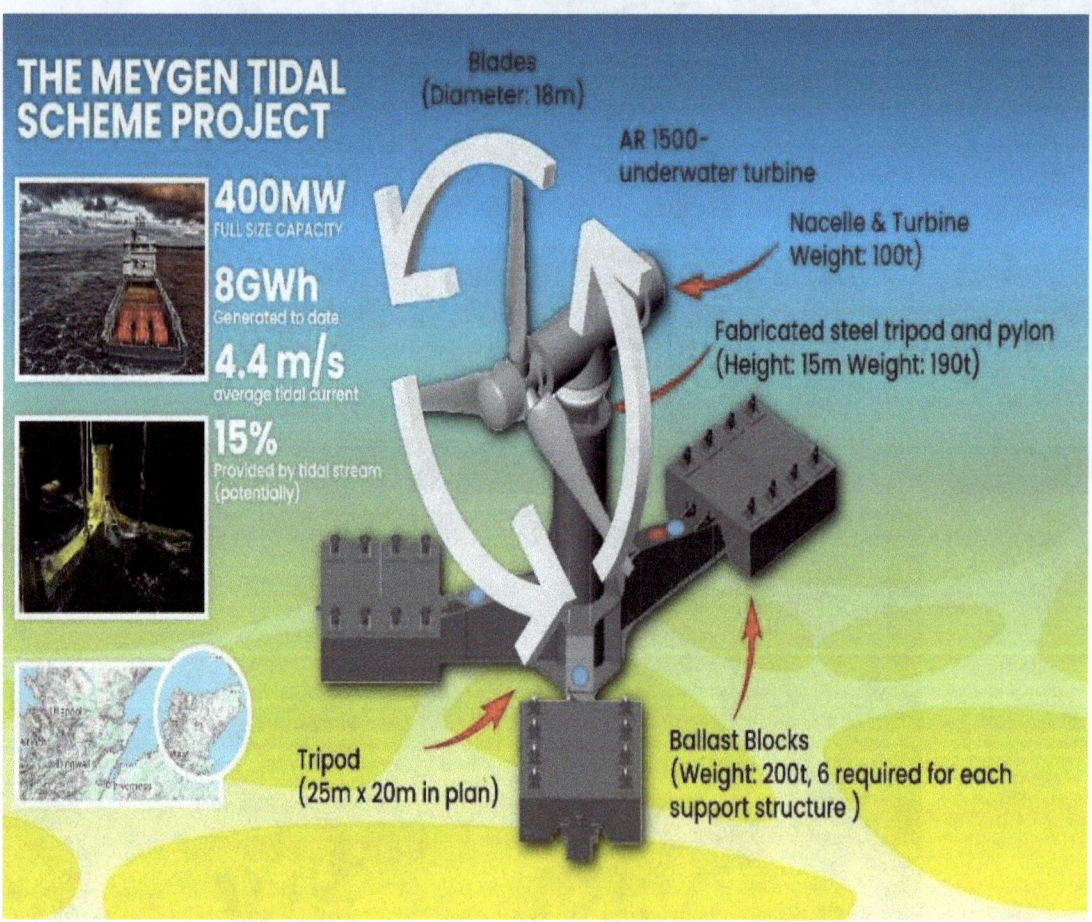

Figure 7.4. MeyGen tidal turbines in Scotland.

Challenges and Future Potential

Environmental Impact

One of the significant challenges with tidal energy is its potential impact on marine ecosystems. The construction of tidal barrages and lagoons can disrupt natural water flow, affecting fish migration and sediment transport. However, newer technologies, such as tidal stream generators and floating platforms, have a minimal environmental footprint.

Cost and Scalability

The initial costs of tidal energy projects are high due to the complex engineering and construction required. However, with technological advancements and economies of scale, the costs are expected to decrease, making tidal energy more competitive with other renewable sources.

Future Potential

Tidal energy has enormous potential, particularly in regions with large tidal ranges or strong tidal currents. As technology improves and costs decrease, tidal energy could become a significant contributor to the global energy mix, providing reliable, low-carbon electricity to coastal communities.

Statistical Facts

- **Global Capacity**: As of 2023, the global installed capacity for tidal energy is approximately 600 MW, with significant contributions from France, South Korea, and the United Kingdom.

- **Carbon Savings**: Tidal energy systems can reduce carbon emissions by 20-30 times compared to coal-fired power plants, depending on the technology used.

- **Economic Impact**: The tidal energy sector is projected to create thousands of jobs in engineering, construction, and maintenance as more projects are developed globally.

Hydropower Versus Tidal Energy

Let's quickly explore the difference between these two closely related energy sources.

Tidal energy and hydropower energy are both forms of renewable energy that harness the power of water to generate electricity, but they do so in different ways and under different conditions. Here is a detailed comparison:

1. Source of Energy

- **Tidal Energy:** Tidal energy is generated by harnessing the natural rise and fall of ocean tides, which are caused by the gravitational interaction between the Earth, moon, and sun. It captures energy from the movement of water as tides flow in and out.

- **Hydropower Energy:** Hydropower, or hydroelectric energy, is generated by capturing the energy of flowing or falling water, typically from rivers, streams, or dams. It relies on the gravitational force of falling or flowing water to spin turbines and generate electricity.

2. Location

- **Tidal Energy:** Tidal energy systems are typically located along coastlines or at the mouths of large rivers where tidal movements are strong. Ideal locations are areas with a significant tidal range (the difference between high and low tide).

- **Hydropower Energy:** Hydropower plants are usually built near large rivers or water bodies, often requiring the construction of a dam to create a reservoir of water that can be released to generate power. Hydropower can also be generated by rivers and streams without dams in what are called run-of-river systems.

3. Predictability

- **Tidal Energy:** Tidal energy is highly predictable because tidal patterns are consistent and can be forecasted years in advance. This makes tidal energy a reliable source of power, albeit only available at specific times of the day.

- **Hydropower Energy:** Hydropower is also reliable but depends on consistent water flow, which can be affected by seasonal variations, droughts, and climate change. However, with dam-based systems, power generation can be more controllable.

4. Environmental Impact

- **Tidal Energy:** The environmental impact of tidal energy can include disruption to marine ecosystems, particularly in the case of tidal barrages, which can alter water flow, sediment movement, and fish migration patterns. However, newer technologies like tidal stream generators have a lower environmental footprint.

- **Hydropower Energy:** Hydropower can have significant environmental impacts, especially when large dams are involved. These impacts include altering river ecosystems, disrupting fish migration, displacing communities, and affecting water quality. However, run-of-river systems have less environmental impact compared to large dam-based hydropower plants.

5. Energy Conversion Technology

- **Tidal Energy:** Tidal energy conversion typically involves tidal barrages, tidal stream generators, or tidal lagoons. Tidal barrages function like dams but are designed to capture the potential energy of tides. Tidal stream generators work similarly to underwater wind turbines, and tidal lagoons create enclosed areas that capture and release tidal water to generate energy.

- **Hydropower Energy:** Hydropower technology mainly involves dams and turbines. Water stored in a reservoir is released to flow through turbines, generating electricity. In run-of-river systems, flowing water directly turns the turbines without the need for large reservoirs.

6. Cost and Infrastructure

- **Tidal Energy:** Tidal energy projects tend to be expensive to build due to the need for specialized infrastructure in challenging marine environments. However, operational costs can be lower once the system is established, and the energy produced is reliable.

- **Hydropower Energy:** Hydropower plants, especially large dam-based systems, also require significant investment in infrastructure. However, they tend to have long operational lifespans and can produce large amounts of electricity at relatively low ongoing costs.

7. Global Usage

- **Tidal Energy:** Tidal energy is still in the early stages of development and is used on a relatively small scale globally, with a few notable projects in countries like France, South Korea, and the UK.

- **Hydropower Energy:** Hydropower is one of the oldest and most widely used forms of renewable energy, accounting for a significant portion of the world's electricity generation. Major hydropower-producing countries include China, Brazil, Canada, and the United States.

Conclusion

Tidal energy represents a promising, yet underutilized, form of renewable energy. Its predictability and reliability make it an attractive option for generating clean electricity, especially in regions with strong tidal forces. By understanding the technologies and challenges involved, we can appreciate tidal energy's role in a sustainable energy future. As the world continues to seek alternatives to fossil fuels, tidal energy will likely play a crucial role in diversifying our energy sources and reducing our carbon footprint.

While both tidal and hydropower energy harness water's power, they differ in their sources, locations, predictability, environmental impact, and technology. Tidal energy relies on the gravitational pull of the moon and sun, making it predictable but location-specific and still under development. In contrast, hydropower utilizes the flow of rivers or stored water in dams, is widely established, and plays a significant role in global electricity production, but with notable environmental concerns.

Chapter 8

Biomass Energy

Biomass energy harnesses the power of organic materials such as plants, agricultural residues, and animal waste to produce electricity, heat, and biofuels. This renewable energy source is not only abundant but also versatile, offering a way to reduce waste and carbon emissions.

How Biomass Energy Works

Biomass energy transforms organic and inorganic materials into usable energy as shown in Figure 8.1 (a & b). This process can be achieved through two main types of conversions: thermochemical and biochemical.

Let's dive into how each of these processes works.

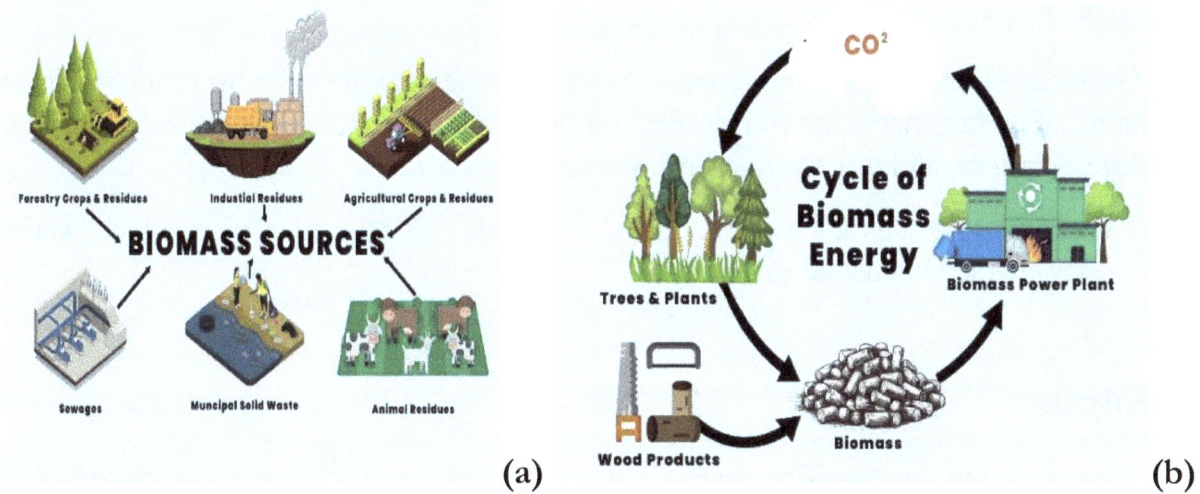

(a) (b)

Figure 8.1.(a&b) Diagram showing sources of biomass and the cycle of biomass energy.

Thermochemical Conversion

Thermochemical conversion involves using heat to break down biomass into energy-rich products. The primary thermochemical processes are combustion, gasification, and pyrolysis. The other three thermochemical processes are hydrothermal liquefaction (HTL), torrefaction, and Hydrothermal Carbonization (HTC).

Combustion

Combustion is the most straightforward method, where biomass is burned to produce heat. This heat can then be used to generate steam, which drives a turbine connected to an electricity generator.

- **Example:** Burning wood chips in a furnace to produce steam that powers an electric generator.

Gasification

Gasification involves heating biomass in a low-oxygen environment to produce syngas, a mixture of hydrogen, carbon monoxide, and carbon dioxide. These syngas can be used to generate electricity, and heat or even be converted into biofuels.

- **Example:** Agricultural waste is heated in a gasifier to produce syngas, which powers a gas engine to generate electricity.

Pyrolysis

Pyrolysis is the process of heating biomass in the absence of oxygen to produce bio-oil, biochar, and syngas. Bio-oil can be refined into fuels, biochar can be used as a soil amendment, and syngas can be used for energy.

- **Example:** Wood chips are heated in a pyrolysis reactor to produce bio-oil, which can be refined into diesel fuel.

Shown in Table 8.1 below is a quick comparison chart for the three thermochemical conversion technologies.

Table 8.1 Combustion, Gasification, and Pyrolysis in Biomass Energy

Aspect	Combustion	Gasification	Pyrolysis
Definition	Complete oxidation of biomass in the presence of excess oxygen to produce heat and flue gases	Partial oxidation of biomass at high temperatures to produce syngas (a mixture of CO, H_2, and CO_2	Thermal decomposition of biomass in the absence of oxygen to produce biochar, bio-oil and syngas.
Temperature Range	800°C -1200°C	700°C -1000°C	400°C -800°C
Oxygen Requirement	Requires excess oxygen for complete combustion.	Requires limited oxygen or air (sub-stoichiometric)	No oxygen is used (Anaerobic conditions).
Main Products	Heat, CO_2, water vapor, and ash.	Syngas (CO, H_2, CO_2), tar, and char.	Biochar, Bio-oil, and Syngas.
Energy Output	Direct heat can be used for electricity generation, heating, or industrial processes.	Syngas can be used for electricity generation, chemical synthesis, or as a fuel.	Bio-oil can be refined into biofuels; Biochar can be used as a soil amendment; Syngas can be burned for heat.
Efficiency	Moderate thermal efficiency; lower compared to gasification and pyrolysis due to heat losses.	Higher efficiency as syngas can be used flexibly for different applications.	High efficiency in terms of product versatility (biochar, bio-oil, and syngas)
Environmental Impact	Higher emissions of CO_2, NOx, and particulate matter. Requires flue gas treatment.	Lower emissions compared to combustion; syngas can be cleaned to reduce pollutants.	Lower emissions; Biochar can sequester carbon, making it environmentally beneficial.
Applications	Power plants, industrial heating, district heating	Flexible energy production, chemical feedstock production, and industrial use.	Production of biofuels, carbon sequestration, soil enhancement, and energy generation.
Advantages	Simple and well established technology; reliable heat generation.	Produces valuable syngas; flexible in energy output; lower emissions.	Produces multiple useful products; potential for carbon sequestration through biochar.
Disadvantages	High emissions; requires extensive flue gas cleaning; less efficient use of biomass	Complex technology; requires careful control of process conditions; tar production can be an issue.	Requires high temperatures and precise control; not all bio-oil is easily upgraded to fuel.

Table 8.1 outlines the key differences between the three main processes used in converting biomass into energy: combustion, gasification, and pyrolysis. Each process shown has distinct advantages and disadvantages depending on the desired energy output, environmental impact, and technological complexity.

Let's quickly explore the differences between the other three thermochemical conversion processes shown in Table 8.2.

Table 8.2 Hydrothermal Liquefaction (HTL), Torrefaction, and Hydrothermal Carbonization

Feature	Hydrothermal Liquefaction (HTL)	Torrefaction	Hydrothermal Carbonization (HTC)
Temperature	250–350°C	200–300°C	180–250°C
Pressure	High pressure (10–20 MPa)	Atmospheric pressure	High pressure (typically 2–5 MPa)
Reaction Environment	Water (subcritical or supercritical)	No water, anaerobic (absence of oxygen)	Water (anaerobic, with high temperature and pressure)
Time	Few hours	Minutes to 1 hour	Several hours
Product Type	Bio-crude oil (liquid), gases, water phase, small solids	Torrefied biomass (solid), gases	Hydrochar (solid), water phase, small gases
Main Product	Bio-crude oil (suitable for biofuel production)	Solid biomass with improved energy density	Hydrochar (solid, coal-like, carbon-rich material)
Feedstock	Suitable for wet biomass (e.g., algae, food waste)	Suitable for dry biomass (e.g., wood, agricultural residues)	Suitable for wet biomass (e.g., food waste, algae, agricultural residues)
Main Application	Biofuel production (liquid fuel)	Biomass upgrading for combustion or gasification	Biomass upgrading for fuel or soil amendment (similar to biochar)

Biochemical Conversion

Biochemical conversion uses microorganisms to break down biomass into energy-rich compounds. The primary biochemical processes are anaerobic digestion and fermentation. These two processes are classified under Hydrolysis. Other Biochemical process is Extraction leading to the production of biodiesel via transesterification process.

Anaerobic Digestion

Anaerobic digestion involves breaking down organic matter in the absence of oxygen to produce biogas, primarily methane and carbon dioxide. This biogas can be used for heating, electricity generation, or as vehicle fuel.

- **Example**: Animal manure is processed in an anaerobic digester to produce biogas, which is used to generate electricity for a farm.

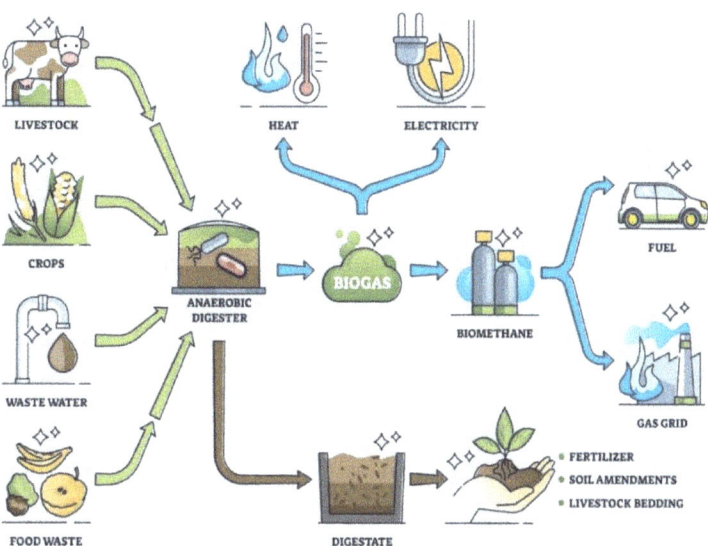

Figure 8.2. Diagram showing the anaerobic digestion process. (Cambi Group, 2025)

Fermentation

Fermentation uses microorganisms to convert biomass into bioethanol and other biofuels. This process typically involves converting sugars and starches found in plants into alcohol, which can be used as fuel.

- **Example:** Corn is fermented by yeast to produce ethanol, which can be blended with gasoline for use in vehicles.

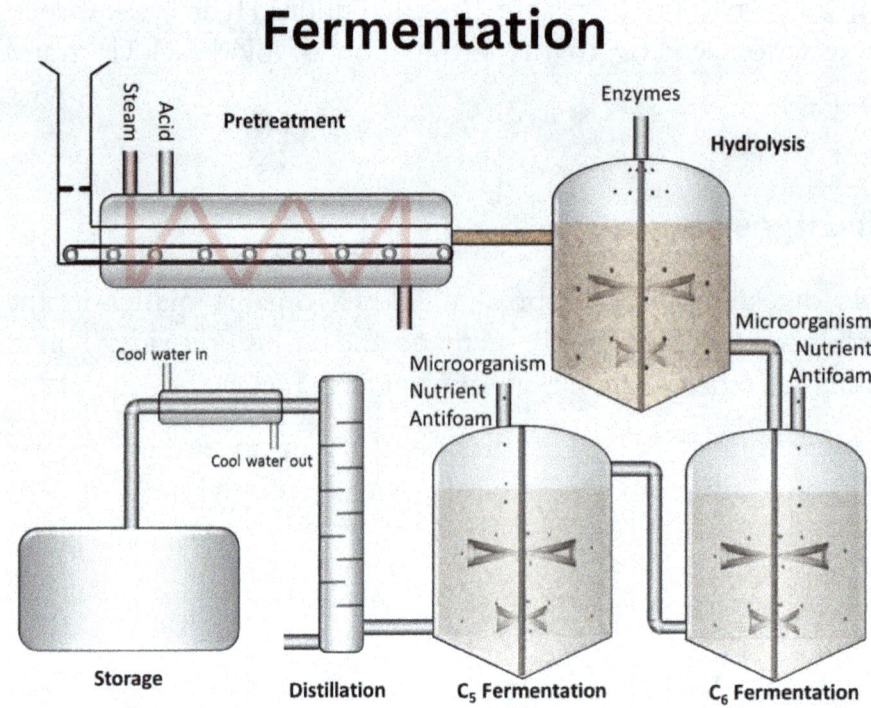

Figure 8.3. Diagram showing the fermentation process (Sonika, 2023)

Table 8.3 shows a quick comparison chart for the primary biochemical conversion technologies.

Table 8.3 Anaerobic Digestion and Fermentation in Biomass Energy

Aspect	Anaerobic Digestion	Fermentation
Definition	A biological process where microorganisms break down organic matter in the absence of oxygen, producing biogas (methane and CO_2) and digestate.	Biological process where microorganisms convert sugars into ethanol, carbon dioxide, and other by-products in the absence of oxygen.
Feedstock	Organic waste (e.g., agricultural waste, food waste, manure, sewage sludge).	Sugary or starchy biomass (e.g., corn, sugarcane, beetroot, cellulosic biomass).
Main Products	Biogas (primarily methane and carbon dioxide) and digestate (a nutrient-rich residue).	Ethanol, carbon dioxide, and by-products such as yeast biomass.
Microorganisms Involved	Methanogenic bacteria (anaerobic microorganisms).	Yeast (typically *Saccharomyces cerevisiae*) or bacteria.

Aspect	Anaerobic Digestion	Fermentation
Oxygen Requirement	Strictly anaerobic (no oxygen present)	Anaerobic but less strict, with some fermentation processes occurring under low oxygen conditions.
End Uses	Biogas is used for electricity generation, and heating, or upgraded to biomethane for use as a vehicle fuel; digestate is used as fertilizer.	Ethanol is used as a biofuel (e.g., in gasoline blends), in alcoholic beverages, or as a chemical feedstock.
Process Conditions	Operates best at mesophilic (20-45°C) or thermophilic (50-60°C) temperatures and neutral pH.	Typically occurs at 30-35°C for yeast fermentation with a neutral to slightly acidic pH.
Timeframe	Relatively slow process, taking several weeks to months for complete digestion.	Relatively fast process, with fermentation taking hours to days depending on the substrate.
Energy Efficiency	High overall energy efficiency, especially when biogas is used for combined heat and power (CHP).	Energy-efficient for ethanol production; residual biomass can be further processed for energy recovery.
Environmental Impact	Reduces methane emissions from organic waste; produces renewable energy and reduces waste volume; digestate can enhance soil health.	Produces renewable fuel (ethanol) with lower greenhouse gas emissions than fossil fuels; some concerns about land use for feedstock production.
Technological Complexity	Moderate; requires well-controlled anaerobic conditions and biogas collection systems.	Moderate to low; well-established technology, particularly in ethanol production industries.
Applications	Waste management, renewable energy production, nutrient recycling in agriculture.	Biofuel production (ethanol), beverage industry, chemical industry.
Advantages	Efficient waste-to-energy conversion; can handle a variety of organic materials; reduces greenhouse gas emissions from waste.	High yield of ethanol from sugar-rich feedstocks; well-established and scalable process; ethanol is a versatile product.
Disadvantages	Requires careful monitoring of anaerobic conditions; biogas upgrading may be necessary for some applications.	Competition with food crops for feedstock; lower energy density of ethanol compared to fossil fuels; land use and sustainability concerns.

Table 8.3 compares the two key biological processes used in biomass energy conversion, highlighting their differences in feedstock, products, process conditions, and environmental impacts. Anaerobic digestion is particularly valued for its waste management capabilities and biogas production, while fermentation is central to bioethanol production, an important biofuel. Figure 8.4 shows the summary of the biomass conversion technologies to energy in the form of heat, electricity, and biofuels.

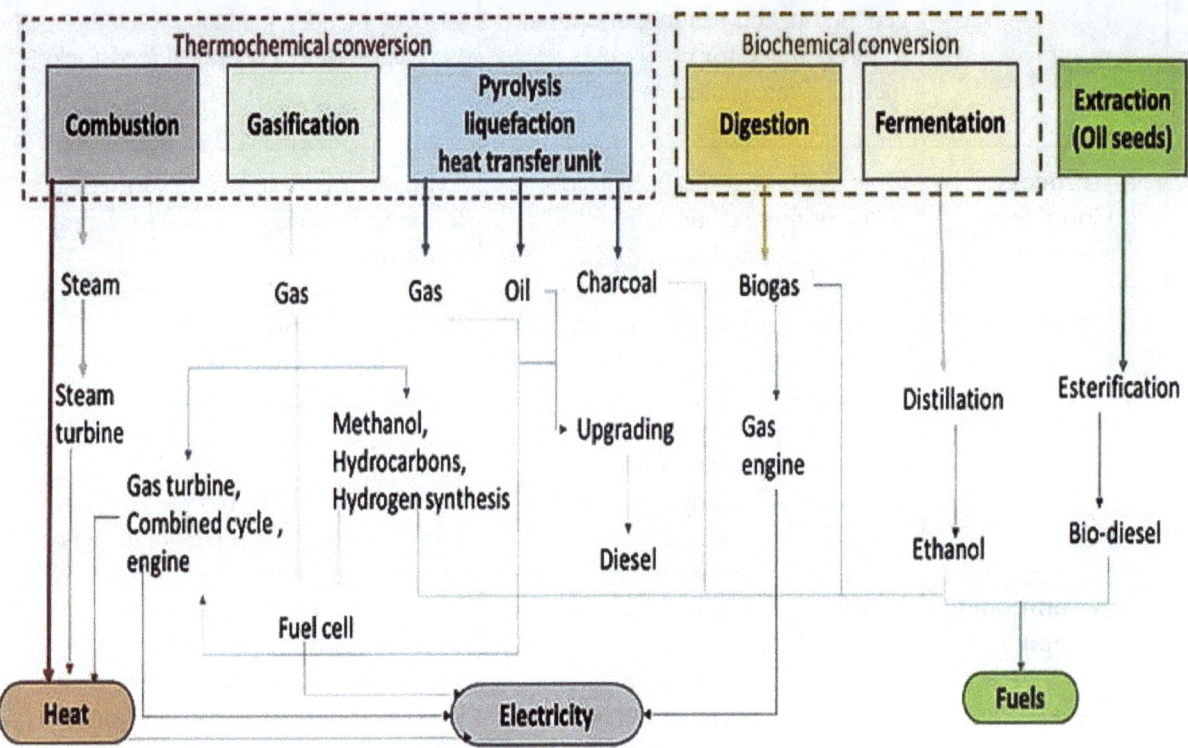

Figure 8.4. Biomass-to-energy conversion pathways (Faaij, 2006)

Technological Advancements

Advanced Biofuels

Second and third-generation biofuels are produced from non-food crops and algae, offering higher yields and lower environmental impacts.

- **Example:** Algae biofuels are being developed as a sustainable alternative to traditional biofuels, with the potential to produce large amounts of energy without competing with food production.

Torrefaction

A thermal process that converts biomass into a coal-like material called bio-coal, which is easier to transport and burn more efficiently.

- **Example:** Wood chips are torrefied to produce bio-coal, which is then used in power plants to reduce carbon emissions.

Integrated Biorefineries

Facilities that process biomass into a range of products, including biofuels, biochemicals, and bioplastics, maximizing the value extracted from biomass.

- **Example:** A biorefinery processes corn stover into ethanol, biogas, and biodegradable plastics, providing multiple revenue streams and reducing waste. An example of an integrated wood biorefinery with several products and by-products, including Biofuel, Biochemicals, Biomaterials, and Electricity, is shown in Figure 8.5.

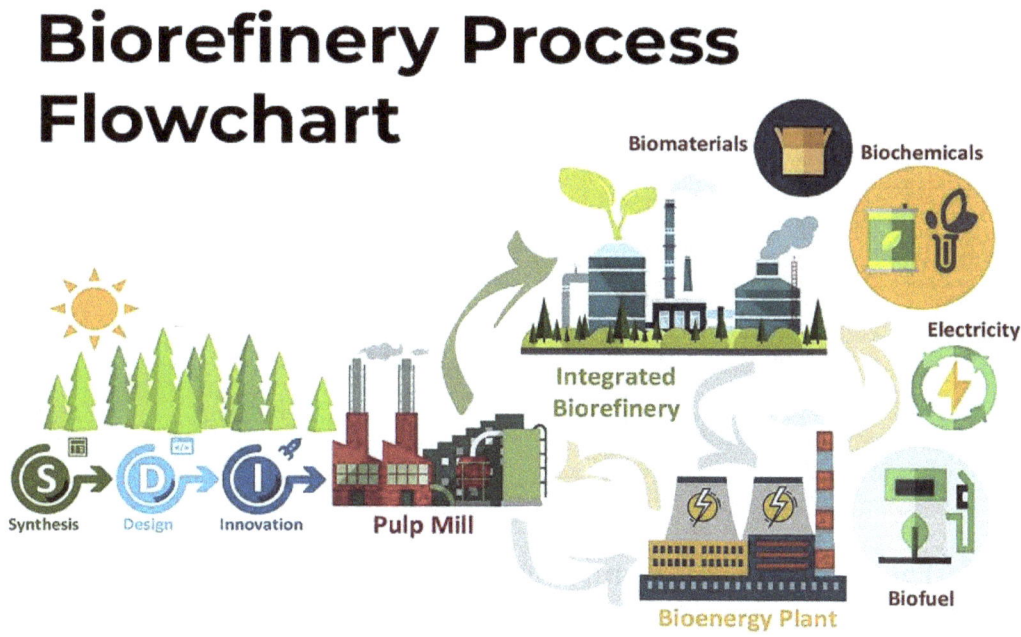

Figure 8.5. Flowchart of an integrated biorefinery process (RBioEnergy, 2024).

Real-Life Success Stories

Denmark's Biomass Heating Systems

Denmark has successfully integrated biomass into its district heating systems, reducing reliance on fossil fuels and lowering greenhouse gas emissions. In cities like Copenhagen, biomass heating plants provide a significant portion of the city's heating needs.

- **Example:** The Amager Bakke plant in Copenhagen uses wood pellets and other biomass to provide electricity and heat to the city, contributing to Denmark's goal of becoming carbon neutral by 2050.

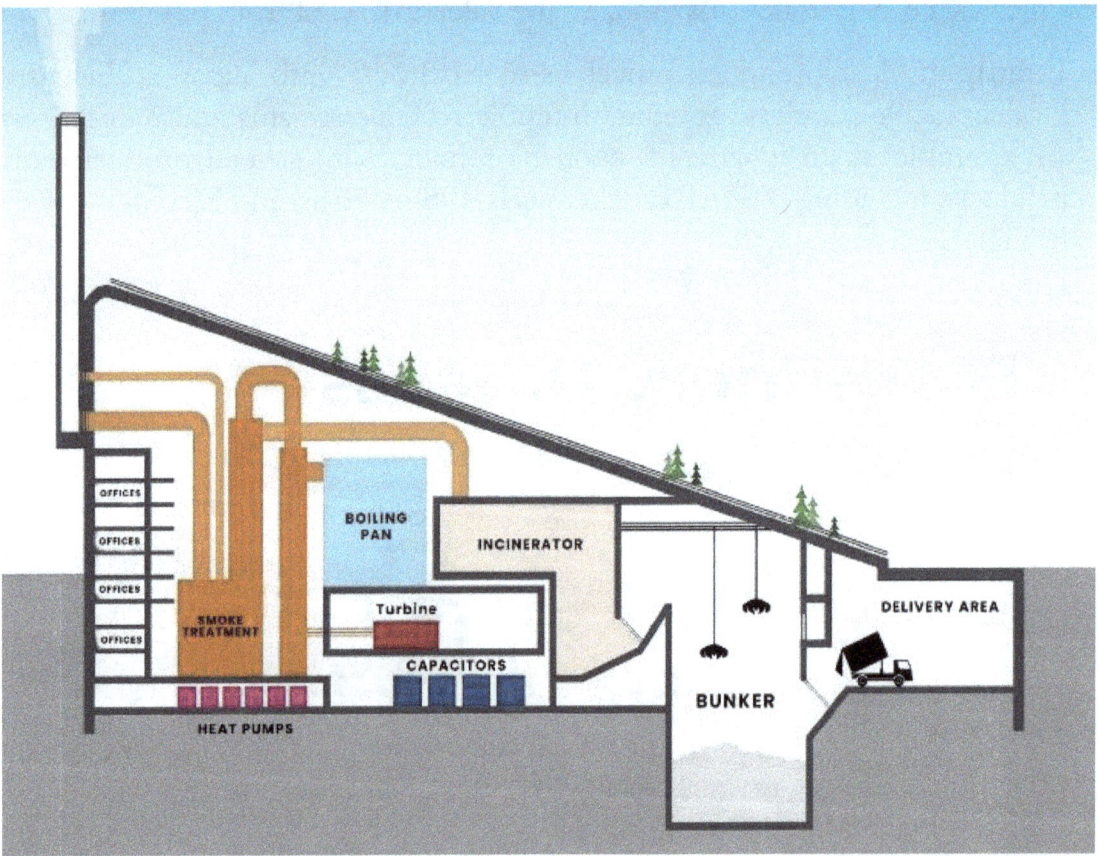

Figure 8.6. The Amager Bakke plant—a combined heat and power plant in Copenhagen.

United States Biomass Power

The United States has numerous biomass power plants that convert agricultural residues, forest by-products, and municipal solid waste into electricity. These plants contribute to energy diversity and waste management.

- **Example:** The E.B. Eddy biomass power plant in Maine uses wood waste to generate electricity, providing a sustainable energy source for the region. Wheelabrator waste-to-energy plant in Baltimore Maryland uses municipal solid waste (commonly called trash) to generate electricity and heat for homes and businesses in the city.

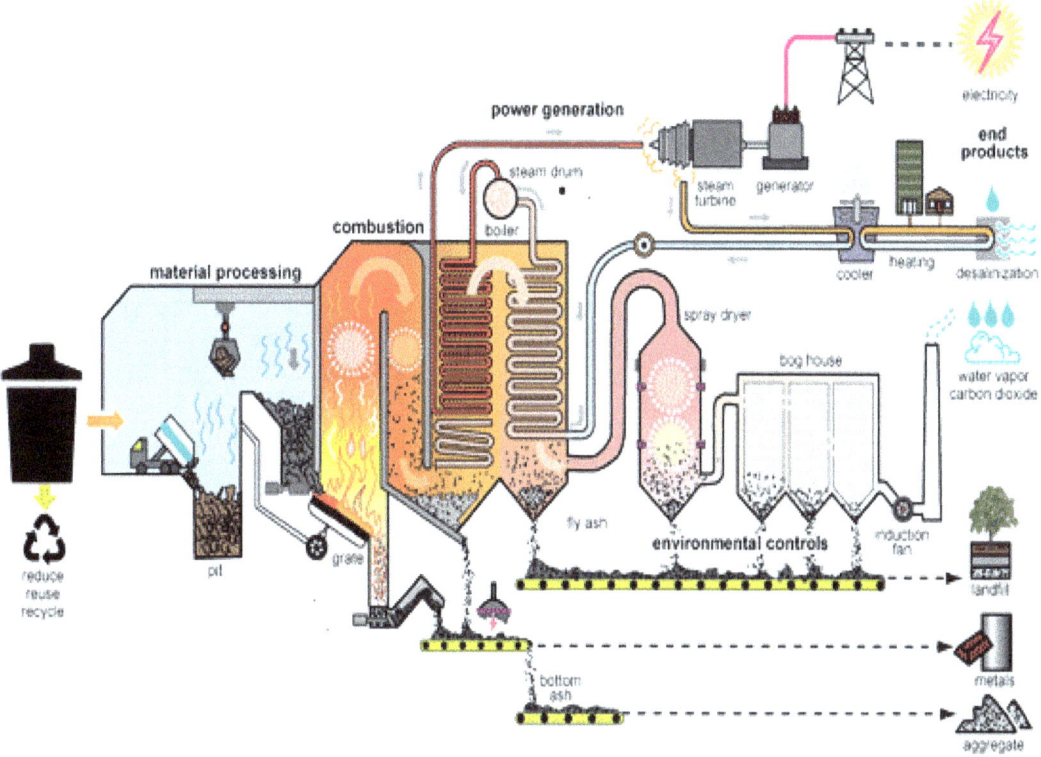

Figure 8.7. A biomass power plant utilizing wood waste for electricity generation (EIA, 2024).

Figures and Statistics

- **Global Capacity:** As of 2023, the global biomass power capacity is around 130 GW, with significant contributions from the United States, China, and Brazil.
- **Carbon Savings:** Biomass energy can reduce carbon emissions by up to 90% compared to fossil fuels, depending on the feedstock and production process.
- **Economic Impact:** The biomass energy sector supports thousands of jobs in agriculture, forestry, and energy production.

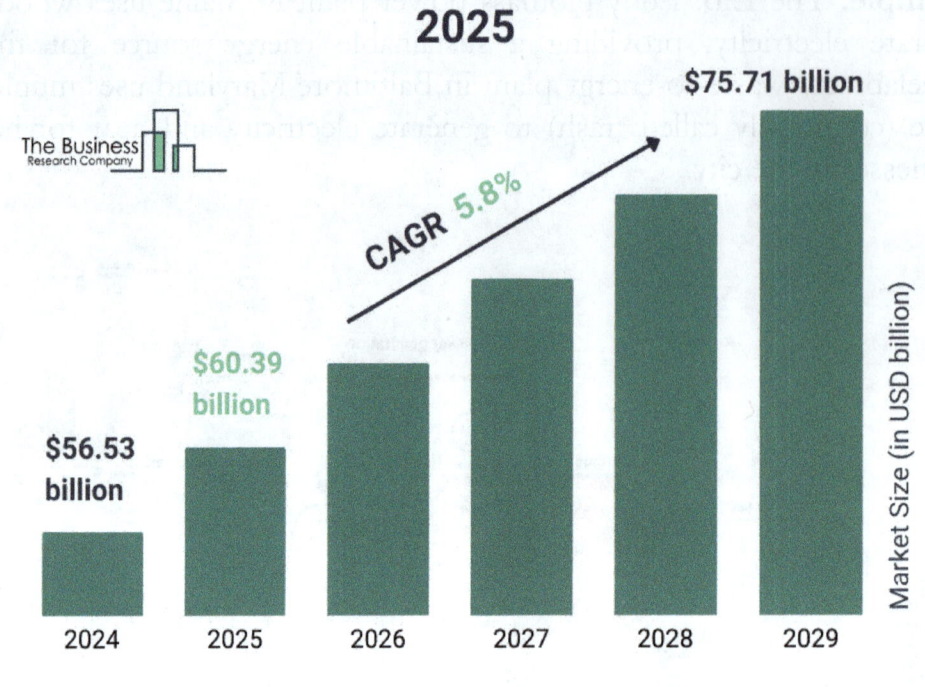

Figure 8.8. Growth of global biomass energy capacity over the years (The Business Research Company, 2025)

Biorefinery in Biomass Energy

A biorefinery is a facility that integrates biomass conversion processes to produce a range of valuable products, including biofuels, bio-based chemicals, and materials, as well as heat and power. Just as a petroleum refinery processes crude oil into multiple products, a biorefinery does the same with biomass, making the most efficient use of all parts of the biomass feedstock. The concept of biorefinery is crucial for the sustainable production of energy and materials as it maximizes the value derived from biomass resources while minimizing waste.

1. Understanding Biorefinery Processes

Biorefineries use a combination of biological, chemical, and thermal processes to break down biomass into its components, which are then refined into various products.

The primary processes include:

- **Pretreatment:** Biomass is first pretreated to make it more amenable to subsequent processing. This might involve mechanical milling, chemical treatment, or thermal processes to break down the structure of the biomass.

- **Conversion Processes**
    - **Thermochemical Conversion:** This includes processes like pyrolysis, gasification, and combustion, which convert biomass into syngas, bio-oil, or heat. The syngas and bio-oil can be further processed into biofuels or chemicals.
    - **Biochemical Conversion:** This involves processes like fermentation, anaerobic digestion, and enzymatic hydrolysis, where microbes or enzymes convert biomass into bioethanol, biogas, or other bio-based products.

- **Separation and Purification:** After conversion, the products are separated and purified to meet the specifications required for their intended uses.

2. Types of Biorefineries

Biorefineries can be categorized based on the type of biomass feedstock they use and the products they generate:

- **First-Generation Biorefineries:** These focus on food crops like corn or sugarcane to produce bioethanol and biodiesel. While effective, these biorefineries often raise concerns about food security and land use.

- **Second-Generation Biorefineries:** These utilize non-food biomass like agricultural residues, wood chips, or grasses. They have the advantage of not competing with food production and can process a broader range of biomass feedstocks.

- **Third-Generation Biorefineries:** These are the most advanced and focus on innovative feedstocks like algae. Algal biorefineries are particularly promising because algae can produce high yields of biofuels and other products without the need for arable land.

3. Products from Biorefineries

Biorefineries produce a wide array of products, classified broadly into the following categories:

- **Biofuels:** These include ethanol, biodiesel, biogas, and advanced biofuels like biojet fuel (also known as Sustainable Aviation Fuel). Biofuels are crucial for reducing greenhouse gas emissions in the transportation sector.

- **Biochemicals:** These are chemicals derived from biomass that can replace petroleum- based chemicals. Examples include bio-based plastics, solvents, and fertilizers.

- **Bio-based Materials:** Biorefineries also produce materials like biodegradable plastics, fibers, and resins, which are used in packaging, textiles, and construction.

- **Power and Heat:** By utilizing every part of the biomass, biorefineries can also generate electricity and heat, often used to power the facility itself or sold to the grid.

4. Technological Advancements

Recent advancements in biorefinery technologies have focused on increasing efficiency, reducing costs, and expanding the range of feedstocks and products:

- **Integrated Biorefineries:** These facilities combine multiple conversion processes, enabling them to produce a broader range of products from the same biomass feedstock.

- **Advanced Catalysts:** New catalysts are being developed to improve the efficiency of chemical conversions in biorefineries, making it possible to produce higher-value chemicals from biomass.

- **Genetically Engineered Microorganisms:** Biotechnology plays a significant role in enhancing the biochemical conversion processes. Genetically engineered microbes can be tailored to produce specific chemicals more efficiently from biomass.

5. Benefits of Biorefineries

- **Sustainability:** Biorefineries contribute to a circular economy by converting waste and non-food biomass into valuable products, reducing reliance on fossil fuels, and lowering greenhouse gas emissions.

- **Economic Growth:** The development of biorefineries can stimulate rural economies by providing new markets for agricultural residues and creating jobs in biomass processing and product manufacturing.

- **Energy Security:** By diversifying the sources of energy and materials, biorefineries enhance energy security, reducing dependence on imported fossil fuels.

6. Challenges and Future Prospect

While biorefineries offer significant potential, they also face challenges:

- **High Initial Costs:** The development of biorefineries requires significant investment in infrastructure and technology, which can be a barrier to entry.
- **Feedstock Availability:** The availability and consistency of biomass feedstock are critical factors that can affect the viability of biorefineries.
- **Technological Complexity:** The integration of multiple processes in a biorefinery is technologically complex and requires ongoing innovation to remain competitive.

Despite these challenges, the future of biorefineries is promising. With continued advancements in technology and increased emphasis on sustainability, biorefineries are expected to play a crucial role in the transition to a bio-based economy.

Biorefineries represent the cutting edge of biomass energy, turning renewable resources into a wide array of products that can help meet the world's energy, material, and environmental needs. By understanding the processes and technologies behind biorefineries, students can appreciate their potential to drive a sustainable future.

Below in Table 8.4 is a chart that provides a comparative overview of the key differences between biorefineries and fossil fuel refineries, highlighting their feedstocks, environmental impact, processing techniques, and economic considerations.

Table 8.4 Biorefinery vs. Fossil Fuel Refinery

Aspect	Biorefinery	Fossil Fuel Refinery
Feedstock	Biomass (e.g., agricultural residues, wood, algae)	Crude oil and natural gas
Primary Products	Biofuels, biochemicals, bio-based materials, electricity	Gasoline, diesel, jet fuel, petrochemicals
Sustainability	Renewable and often carbon-neutral or low-carbon	Non-renewable and high carbon emissions

Aspect	Biorefinery	Fossil Fuel Refinery
Environmental Impact	Lower greenhouse gas emissions, biodegradable products	Significant greenhouse gas emissions, pollution
Processing Techniques	Thermochemical (e.g., pyrolysis, gasification, combustion), biochemical (e.g., fermentation, anaerobic digestion)	Thermal cracking, catalytic reforming, hydrocracking.
Energy Efficiency	Emerging technologies are improving efficiency	High efficiency due to mature technologies
By-products	Biodegradable waste, organic fertilizers	Hazardous waste, CO_2 emissions, sulfur compounds
Economic Viability	High initial costs, but potential for diversified products and rural economic growth	High profitability but subject to oil market volatility
Scalability	Still developing, with advancements needed for large-scale deployment	Highly scalable with established global infrastructure
Global Presence	Growing presence, with significant adoption in Europe and North America	Extensive global presence with vast networks of refineries

Conclusion

Biomass energy offers a sustainable solution for waste management and renewable energy production. With advancements in technology and an increasing focus on reducing carbon emissions, biomass has the potential to play a significant role in the global energy transition. By understanding how biomass energy works and its benefits and challenges, we can better appreciate its place in the renewable energy landscape.

Chapter 9

Geothermal Energy

Geothermal energy is a fascinating and vital source of renewable energy that taps into the Earth's internal heat. Geothermal energy is the heat stored beneath the Earth's surface. The Earth's core is extremely hot, and this heat slowly rises to the surface, where it can be harnessed for human use. Geothermal energy is considered renewable because the Earth continuously produces heat.

- **Fun Fact**: The word "geothermal" comes from the Greek words "geo" (Earth) and "therme" (heat), meaning "Earth's heat."

How Does Geothermal Energy Work?

Geothermal energy can be captured in different ways, depending on the resource and its temperature:

- **Geothermal Power Plants:** These plants are usually located in areas with high geothermal activity, like near volcanoes or hot springs. They work by drilling wells into the Earth's crust to access hot water and steam, which then spins a turbine connected to a generator to produce electricity.

- **Direct Use Applications:** Geothermal heat can be used directly to heat buildings, grow crops in greenhouses, or dry crops. This is a very efficient use of geothermal energy because it skips the conversion to electricity.

- **Geothermal Heat Pumps:** These pumps use stable temperatures near the Earth's surface to heat and cool buildings. They work by circulating a fluid through a loop of pipes buried in the ground. In winter, the fluid absorbs heat from the ground and brings it into the building; in summer, the system removes heat from the building and deposits it in the cooler ground.

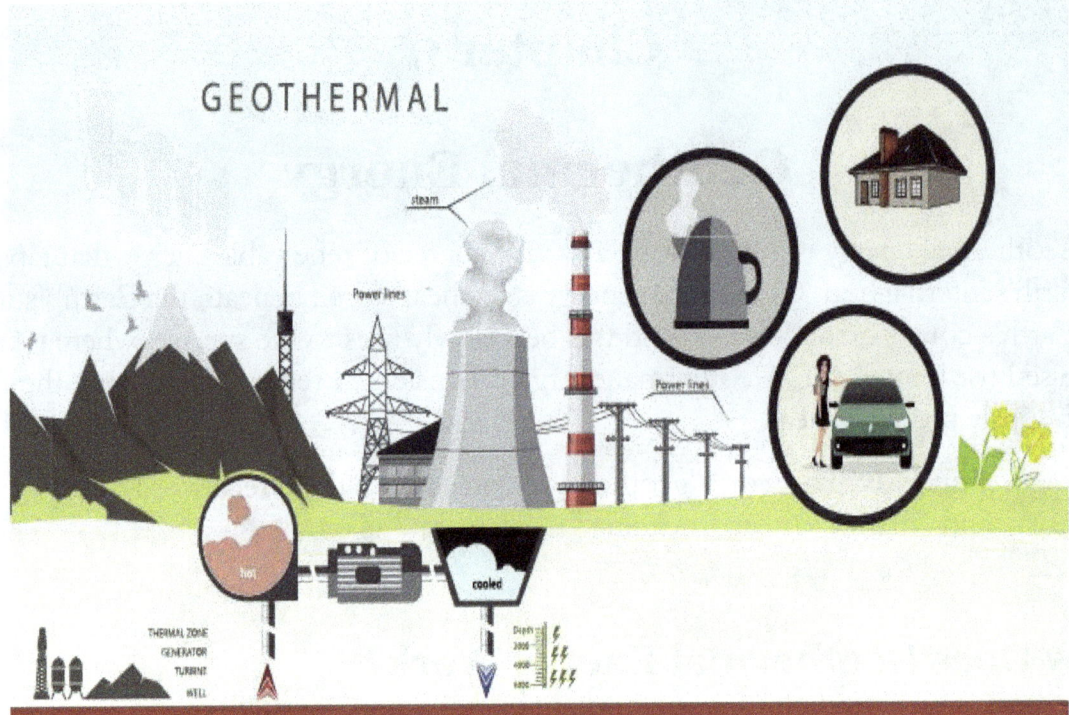

Figure 9.1. Illustration of geothermal energy

Technological Advancements in Geothermal Energy

- **Enhanced Geothermal Systems (EGS)**: Traditional geothermal energy extraction relies on naturally occurring hot water or steam. EGS, however, creates artificial reservoirs in hot dry rock formations by injecting water into them. This water heats up and is then pumped back to the surface to generate electricity.

- **Supercritical Geothermal**: This cutting-edge technology involves drilling even deeper into the Earth to reach "supercritical" fluids, which are neither liquid nor gas but can carry much more energy. These fluids can generate more electricity from smaller quantities of water.

- **Binary Cycle Power Plants**: These are newer geothermal plants that can operate with lower temperature resources. They use a secondary fluid with a lower boiling point than water, which is vaporized by geothermal heat and used to drive a turbine.

Benefits of Geothermal Energy

Geothermal energy has several advantages that make it an attractive option for clean energy:

- **Reliability:** Unlike solar or wind energy, geothermal energy doesn't depend on the weather. It can provide a constant and stable supply of energy, 24/7.

- **Low Emissions:** Geothermal power plants emit very little carbon dioxide or other greenhouse gases. In fact, their emissions are often comparable to those of wind power.

- **Small Land Footprint:** Geothermal plants require much less land compared to solar or wind farms, making them ideal for areas where land is scarce.

Challenges of Geothermal Energy

While geothermal energy has many benefits, it also faces some challenges:

- **Location-Specific:** Geothermal resources are not available everywhere. They are most found in regions with high tectonic activity, like the Pacific Ring of Fire.

- **High Initial Costs:** Drilling deep into the Earth to access geothermal resources can be expensive. The upfront costs of building a geothermal plant are higher than those for solar or wind, although the long-term operating costs are lower.

- **Induced Seismicity:** Sometimes, the process of drilling and injecting water into the Earth can cause minor earthquakes. While these are usually small, they can be a concern in certain areas.

Real-World Examples

- **Iceland:** Nearly 90% of Iceland's homes are heated using geothermal energy. The country is a global leader in geothermal power, thanks to its abundant geothermal resources.

- **The Geysers, California:** The Geysers is the largest geothermal power complex in the world, located in Northern California. It generates enough electricity to power about 725,000 homes.

- **Global Geothermal Capacity:** As of the most recent data, the world has over 15 GW of installed geothermal power capacity. Countries like the United States, Indonesia, and the Philippines are major producers.

Conclusion

Geothermal energy is a powerful and reliable source of renewable energy with the potential to play a significant role in the global transition to sustainable energy. With ongoing technological advancements, it is likely that geothermal energy will become an even more important part of our energy future. Understanding geothermal energy will help you appreciate the innovative ways we can harness the Earth's natural heat to power our world.

Chapter 10

From Power Plant to Plug — How Electricity Gets to You

Electricity powers your phone, your lights, your school, and your world. But have you ever wondered how it travels from the power plant to your home? This chapter shows how electricity is generated, transmitted, and distributed across the grid and why understanding this journey is key to creating a cleaner energy future.

What Is Electricity Generation?

Electricity starts at a power plant, where a fuel source like coal, natural gas, nuclear, or renewable energy is used to spin a turbine. The turbine is connected to a generator, which converts mechanical energy into electrical energy through a process called electromagnetic induction.

Types of Power Plants

- **Solar Farms** – Use sunlight to generate electricity with photovoltaic (PV) cells.
- **Wind Turbines** – Capture wind to spin a rotor and create electricity.
- **Hydropower Dams** – Use flowing water to spin turbines.
- **Thermal Plants** – Burn coal, natural gas, or biomass to produce steam that turns turbines.
- **Geothermal Plants** – Use underground heat to produce steam and spin turbines.
- **Nuclear Power Plants** – Use heat from nuclear reactions (fission) to boil water and create steam that spins turbines.

Let's look at the steps involved in delivering electricity to your homes, schools, or commercial centers.

Step 1: Generation (Where Electricity Begins)

Once the generator creates electricity, it is usually in the form of alternating current

(AC), which is ideal for traveling long distances. At this stage, the electricity is at a lower voltage — not yet ready for the long journey ahead.

Step 2: Transmission (The Highway System)

Before it can travel far, the voltage of electricity must be increased using a step-up transformer. High-voltage electricity travels more efficiently and with less loss over long distances.

- These transmission lines run across metal towers and cover hundreds of miles.
- They carry electricity at tens or hundreds of thousands of volts.
- Transmission lines link regional power plants with substations closer to where people live.

Did You Know? Some high-voltage transmission lines can carry electricity at over 500,000 volts (500 kV)!

Step 3: Distribution (The Local Delivery System)

When electricity gets closer to homes and businesses, it needs to be stepped down to a safer, lower voltage:

- Substations use step-down transformers to reduce voltage.
- From substations, distribution lines carry electricity into neighborhoods.
- You may see them on utility poles or buried underground.
- Transformers on poles or near buildings reduce voltage one last time so it's safe to use in homes (around 120–240 volts in the U.S.).

Step 4: End Use (Plugging In)

Finally, electricity enters your home through your electric meter and flows to your devices (phones, laptops), lighting, and appliances (fridge, AC, microwave, etc.).

The steps highlighted above are shown in Figure 10.1. Your plug is connected to a global system of energy from spinning turbines to your charger cable.

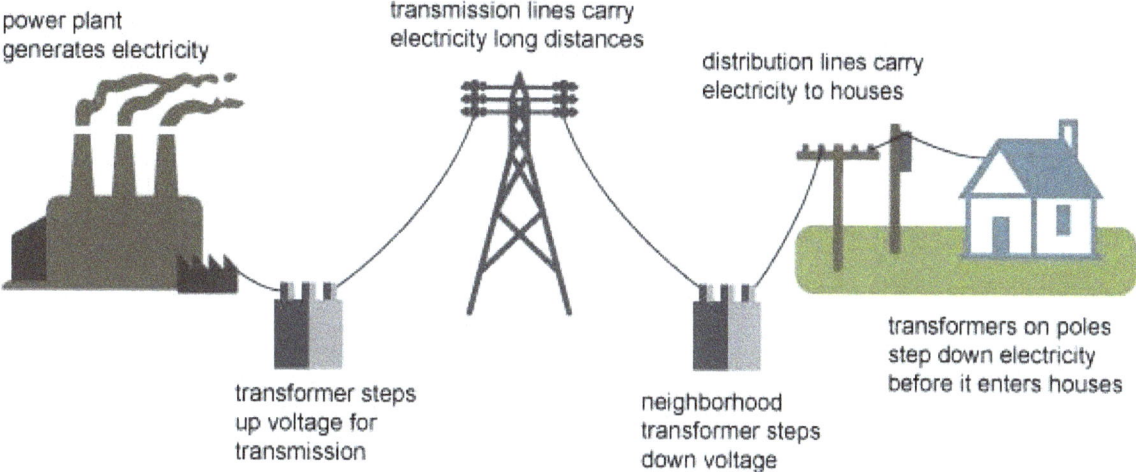

Figure 10.1. Electricity generation, transmission, and distribution (EIA, 2024)

Clean Energy and the Grid

As we transition to more renewable energy, power plants are evolving:

- Solar and wind energy are distributed in smaller units, often closer to where they are used.
- Smart grids are being developed to handle variable renewable energy and support battery storage.
- Microgrids allow schools, communities, and campuses to generate and manage their own electricity locally.

Careers That Keep the Lights On

This system is managed and improved by energy professionals shown in Table 10.1.

Table 10.1 Roles of Energy Professionals in a Power Plant

Career Title	What They Do
Power Plant Operators	Manage generators and ensure electricity is produced safely
Electrical Engineers	Design grid systems and solve technical problems

Career Title	What They Do
Transmission Planners	Design routes for safe, efficient electricity flow
Grid Analysts & Technicians	Monitor and maintain grid operations
Renewable Energy Technicians	Install and repair solar, wind, and storage systems

In summary, electricity is generated at power plants using diverse energy sources (both renewable and non-renewable). It travels over long distances through high-voltage transmission lines before reaching substations, where transformers lower the voltage for safe, local distribution. As clean energy technologies revolutionize this system, you have a vital role to play in shaping the energy future.

Ponder on these:

- What happens when there's a power outage?
- Why do we lose some electricity during transmission?
- How could battery storage or microgrids change the way we use electricity?

Hands-On Activity

"Design Your Own Grid" Challenge: Draw or digitally create a basic map that shows how electricity flows from a solar farm to a school. Include the following:

- Generation source
- Transmission lines
- Substation
- Distribution lines
- End users

Use arrows and labels to explain each step!

Chapter 11

Energy Storage Solutions

Energy storage is a crucial component of modern renewable energy systems, enabling the integration of variable renewable energy sources like solar and wind into the grid. As renewable energy continues to grow, so does the need for effective energy storage solutions that can balance supply and demand, enhance grid stability, and provide backup power.

Energy storage technologies store energy for later use, helping to balance the mismatch between energy generation and consumption. As renewable energy sources are often intermittent, meaning they do not produce energy consistently, energy storage systems (ESS) ensure a reliable supply of electricity by storing excess energy during periods of high generation and releasing it when demand exceeds supply.

Types of Energy Storage Technologies

Batteries

- **Lithium-Ion Batteries**: Lithium-ion batteries are the most widely used type of battery storage due to their high energy density, efficiency, and declining costs. Figure 11.1 shows the current and future market size of Lithium-ion battery. They are prevalent in residential solar energy systems, electric vehicles, and large-scale grid storage.

- **Flow Batteries**: Flow batteries, such as vanadium redox batteries (VRB), are suitable for large-scale energy storage. They have a longer lifespan than lithium-ion batteries and can discharge energy over extended periods, making them ideal for grid stabilization.

- **Lead-Acid Batteries**: Although an older technology, Lead-Acid batteries are still used in certain applications, particularly in off-grid and backup power systems, due to their low cost.

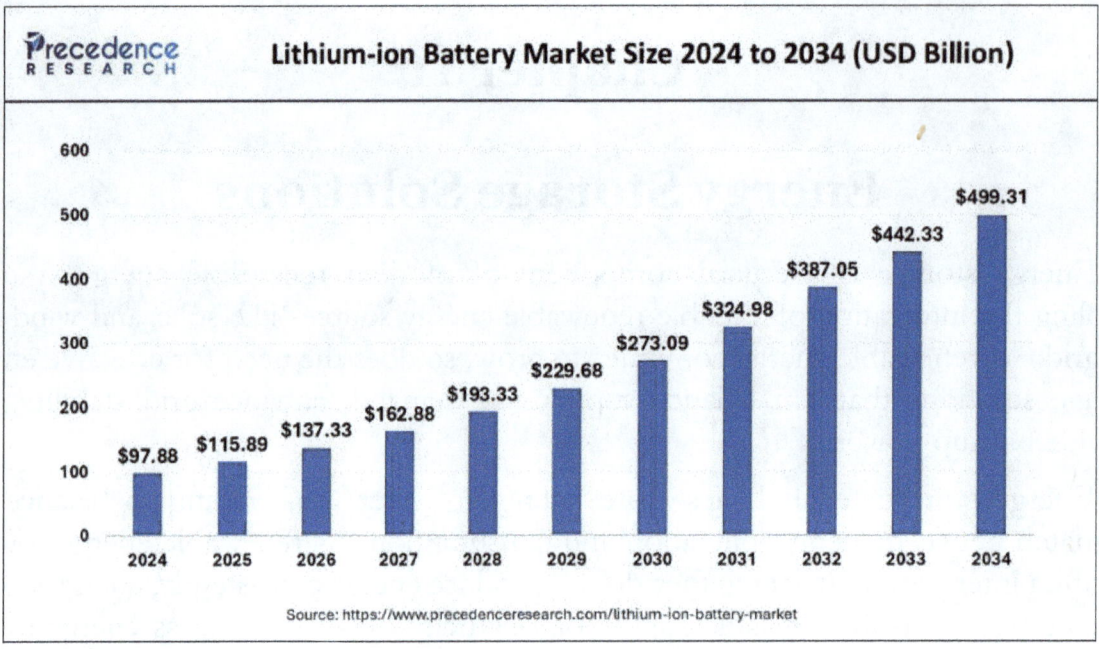

Figure 11.1. Growth in lithium-ion battery market share (Zoting, 2025)

Mechanical Storage

- **Pumped Hydroelectric Storage**: This is the most widely used form of large-scale energy storage, accounting for over 90% of the world's storage capacity. Water is pumped to a higher elevation during periods of excess electricity and released to generate electricity when needed. This technology is shown in Figure 11.2 for a typical pumped hydroelectric power plant.

- **Flywheels**: Flywheel energy storage systems store energy by spinning a rotor at high speeds. They are highly efficient, with fast response times, making them suitable for frequency regulation and grid stability.

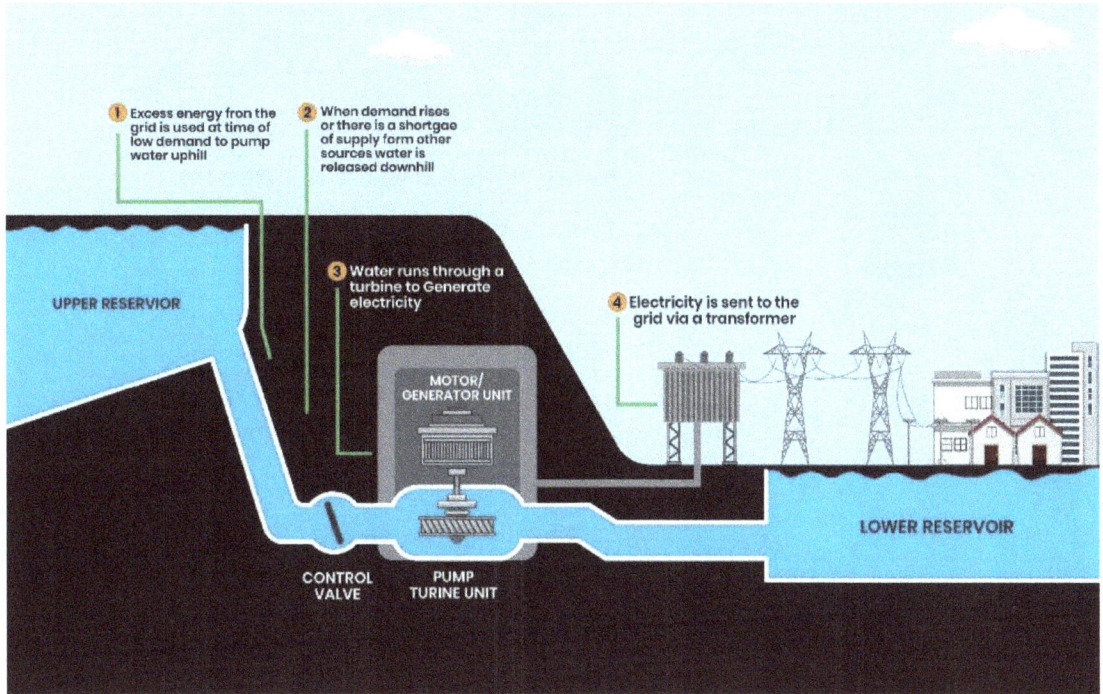

Figure 11.2. Pumped hydroelectric storage power plant

Thermal Storage

- **Molten Salt Storage**: Used primarily in concentrated solar power (CSP) plants, molten salt stores thermal energy at high temperatures, which can then be used to generate electricity when the sun is not shining.

- **Ice Storage**: Ice storage systems use electricity to freeze water at night when demand is low and then use the ice for cooling during the day, reducing peak electricity demand.

Hydrogen Storage

Hydrogen as an Energy Carrier: Excess electricity can be used to produce hydrogen through electrolysis. The hydrogen can then be stored and used in fuel cells or burned to generate electricity when needed, providing a long-duration storage solution as shown in Figure 11.3.

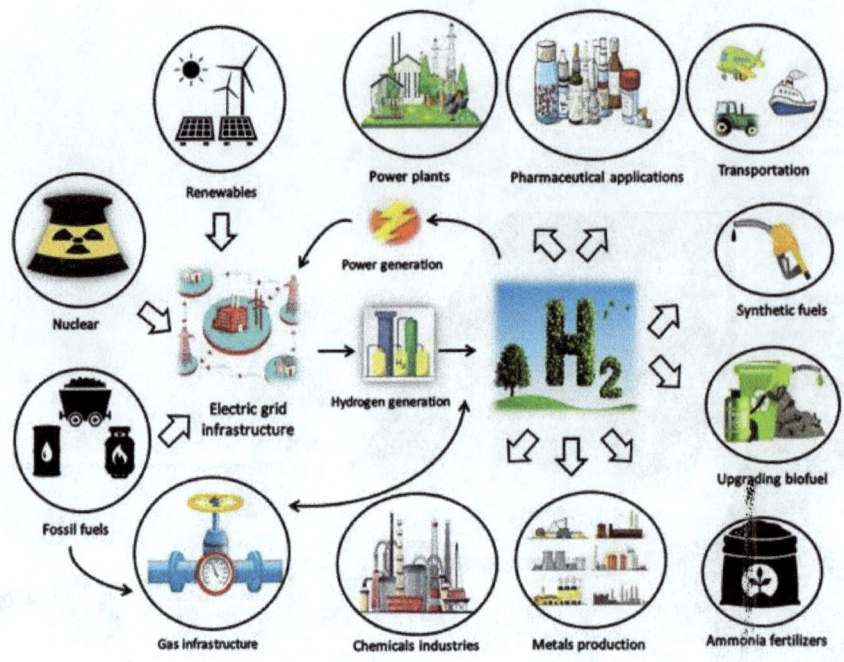

Figure 11.3. Hydrogen production and storage pathways (Osman et al., 2022)

Applications of Energy Storage

- **Grid Stabilization**: Energy storage helps balance supply and demand on the grid, providing frequency regulation, voltage support, and black start capabilities.

- **Renewable Energy Integration**: ESS enables the integration of large amounts of renewable energy by storing excess power and supplying it during periods of low generation.

- **Backup Power**: In residential and commercial settings, energy storage systems provide backup power during outages, ensuring continuous operation of critical systems.

- **Electric Vehicles (EVs)**: Batteries are central to the operation of EVs, and advancements in battery technology are driving the adoption of electric transportation.

Figure 11.4 shows the energy storage system with the technologies on the left and the applications on the right-side. The energy storage technologies are Batteries, Ultracapacitors, Flywheels, superconducting magnetic energy storage (SEMS), Pump Hydro Energy, Compressed Air Energy.

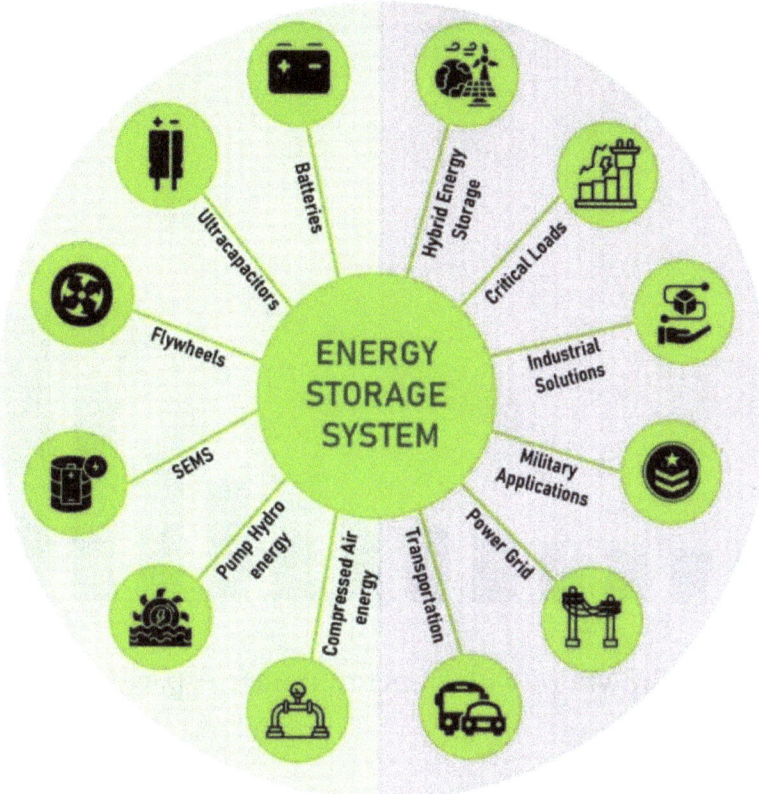

Figure 11.4. Applications of energy storage in different sectors (Aghmadi & Mohammed, 2024)

Latest Technological Advancements

- **Solid-State Batteries**: Solid-state batteries represent the next generation of battery technology, offering higher energy densities, improved safety, and longer lifespans compared to traditional lithium-ion batteries. They are still in the development stage but have the potential to revolutionize energy storage.

- **Second-Life Batteries**: As EV batteries reach the end of their useful life in vehicles, they can be repurposed for stationary energy storage, providing a cost-effective and sustainable solution for grid storage.

- **Advanced Grid Management**: Artificial intelligence (AI) and machine learning (ML) are being integrated into energy storage systems to optimize their operation, predict energy demand, and manage distributed energy resources (DERs) more effectively.

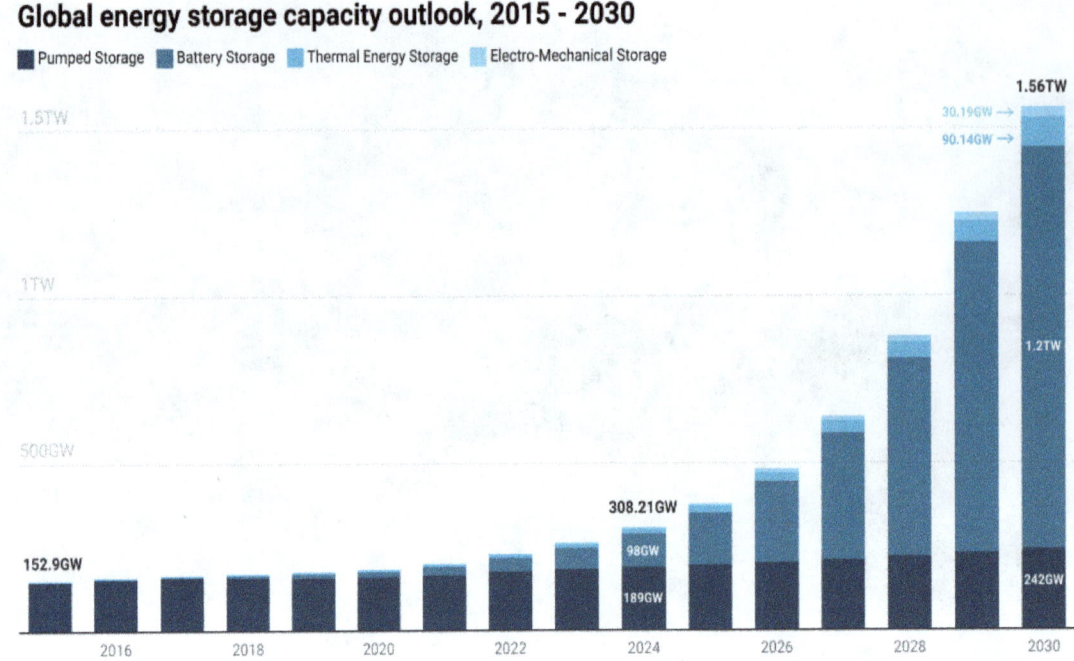

Figure 11.5. Growth of global energy storage capacity (Park, 2024)

Challenges and Future Prospects

- **Cost Reduction**: While costs have been declining, further reductions in the cost of energy storage technologies, particularly batteries, are necessary to achieve widespread adoption.

- **Scalability**: Scaling up energy storage to meet the demands of a fully renewable grid presents technical and economic challenges that require ongoing innovation and investment.

- **Policy and Regulation**: Supportive policies and regulatory frameworks are essential to incentivize the deployment of energy storage and ensure its integration into the energy market.

The Role of Lithium-Ion Batteries in Electric Vehicle Manufacturing

Lithium-ion batteries are at the heart of the electric vehicle (EV) revolution. These batteries are what make electric cars run smoothly, providing the power needed to drive long distances without emitting harmful gases like traditional gasoline cars.

Let's dive into how these batteries work and why they are so important in today's world of transportation.

What are Lithium-Ion Batteries?

Lithium-ion (Li-ion) batteries are rechargeable batteries that store energy by moving lithium ions between a positive electrode (cathode) and a negative electrode (anode). When the battery is charging, lithium ions move from the cathode to the anode. When the battery is discharging, or being used to power the car, the ions move back from the anode to the cathode, releasing energy that powers the vehicle.

These batteries are preferred for EVs because they can store a lot of energy in a small space (high energy density), are lightweight, and can be recharged many times.

Advancements in Lithium-Ion Batteries Technology

Recent advancements have made lithium-ion batteries even more powerful and efficient for use in electric vehicles. Here are some of the latest developments:

- **High-Energy Cathodes**: Scientists have improved the cathode materials in lithium-ion batteries by adding more nickel, which increases the battery's energy density. This means that EVs can now travel longer distances on a single charge.

- **Fast Charging**: New technologies allow these batteries to charge much faster than before. For example, some EVs can now be charged to 80% of their capacity in just 30 minutes, which is roughly the time it takes to have a quick meal at a rest stop.

- **Solid-State Batteries**: A big innovation on the horizon is the development of solid-state batteries. Instead of using a liquid or gel electrolyte, these batteries use a solid electrolyte, which makes them safer (less risk of catching fire) and even more energy-dense. Though still in development, they are expected to greatly enhance the performance and safety of EVs.

Why Lithium-Ion Batteries Are Important for EVs

- **Efficiency**: Lithium-ion batteries are very efficient, meaning they can convert a high percentage of the energy they store into usable power for the car. This helps EVs travel further without needing to recharge.

- **Environmental Benefits**: Unlike gasoline engines, which burn fossil fuels and release carbon dioxide (CO_2), EVs with lithium-ion batteries produce no direct emissions. This is a huge benefit in the fight against climate change.

- **Cost Reduction**: As technology has improved, the cost of lithium-ion batteries has decreased significantly. This has made electric vehicles more affordable for consumers and more competitive with traditional cars.

Real-World Impact and Future Trends

The adoption of lithium-ion batteries in electric vehicles has skyrocketed in recent years. Major car manufacturers like Tesla, Nissan, and Ford are using these batteries to power their EVs, contributing to the millions of electric vehicles on the roads today.

In the future, we can expect even more exciting developments, such as:

- **Increased Range**: As battery technology continues to improve, electric cars will be able to travel even longer distances without needing to recharge.
- **Second-Life Batteries**: After batteries are no longer suitable for use in cars, they can be repurposed for other applications, like storing renewable energy for homes or businesses.
- **Sustainability**: Companies are working on recycling methods to recover valuable materials from used batteries, reducing waste, and making the production process more sustainable.

Statistical Facts

- **Battery Range**: Modern EVs can travel anywhere from 200 to over 400 miles on a single charge, thanks to advancements in lithium-ion battery technology.
- **Charging Speed**: Some EVs can achieve 80% charge in under 30 minutes with fast-charging stations, making long-distance travel more convenient.
- **Cost**: The cost of lithium-ion batteries has dropped by nearly 89% over the past decade, making electric vehicles more accessible.

Lithium-ion batteries are transforming how we think about transportation, paving the way for a cleaner, more sustainable future. As technology continues to evolve, these batteries will play an even bigger role in making electric vehicles the standard mode of transportation around the world.

Conclusion

Energy storage plays a pivotal role in achieving a sustainable energy future by supporting the stable and efficient integration of renewable energy sources into the power grid. The continued development and deployment of advanced energy storage technologies will be critical in addressing the challenges of climate change and transitioning to a low-carbon energy system. As the market for energy storage grows, so too does the potential for innovation, making it an exciting and dynamic field for future engineers, scientists, and policymakers.

Chapter 12

The Future of Renewable Energy

As the world transitions from fossil fuels to more sustainable energy sources, the future of renewable energy looks brighter than ever. Governments, industries, and communities worldwide are increasing their focus on clean, renewable energy solutions to combat climate change, reduce pollution, and ensure energy security. Let's explore the potential growth areas in renewable energy, including technological advancements, market trends, and global initiatives. The future of renewable energy is shaped by innovations in solar, wind, hydro, geothermal, biomass, and emerging energy sources like hydrogen, as well as critical energy storage and smart grid technologies.

Key Trends in Renewable Energy

The growth in renewable energy is influenced by several global trends:

- **Global Decarbonization Goals**: Countries are setting ambitious goals to reduce greenhouse gas emissions and shift toward net-zero carbon economies. The Paris Agreement, which aims to limit global warming to 1.5°C, has encouraged nations to adopt clean energy policies.

- **Declining Costs**: The costs of solar panels, wind turbines, and batteries have dropped significantly in the past decade. According to the International Renewable Energy Agency (IRENA), the cost of solar photovoltaics (PV) fell by 85% between 2010 and 2020, while wind energy saw a 56% decline.

- **Electrification of Transportation and Industry**: The adoption of electric vehicles (EVs) and electrified industrial processes is driving demand for renewable energy. As more industries seek to electrify, the need for green power sources like solar and wind will increase.

Emerging Technologies in Renewable Energy

The future of renewable energy will be shaped by groundbreaking technological innovations that improve efficiency, storage, and integration into existing systems:

- **Solar PV 2.0**: New developments in solar technology, such as bifacial solar panels that capture light from both sides and perovskite solar cells, which promise higher efficiency at a lower cost, will revolutionize solar energy. Floating solar farms are also being deployed on water bodies, reducing land use while harnessing energy from the sun.

- **Offshore Wind Energy**: Offshore wind power is poised for explosive growth, with global capacity expected to expand to 234 gigawatts (GW) by 2030, according to the Global Wind Energy Council. Innovations such as floating wind turbines allow for deployment in deeper waters, significantly increasing the potential for wind energy in coastal regions.

- **Green Hydrogen**: Hydrogen produced using renewable energy, known as green hydrogen, is gaining attention as a clean fuel for industries like steel, shipping, and aviation, which are difficult to decarbonize. Electrolysis, powered by solar or wind, can produce hydrogen without emitting CO_2, making it a key player in the future of energy.

- **Energy Storage**: Battery storage systems are crucial for stabilizing renewable energy grids, especially when wind and solar energy are not consistently available. Advances in lithium-ion battery technology, coupled with emerging storage solutions like solid-state batteries, flow batteries, and even hydrogen storage, will enhance the reliability of renewable energy.

The Role of Smart Grids

Smart grids are transforming how energy is distributed and managed, making it easier to integrate large amounts of renewable energy into the grid. A smart grid uses digital communication technology to monitor and manage energy flow, enabling:

- **Demand Response**: Smart grids can adjust energy consumption based on real-time demand, reducing the need for non-renewable energy sources during peak times.

- **Decentralized Energy Generation**: Microgrids and distributed energy resources, such as rooftop solar panels and small-scale wind turbines, can be connected to the smart grid, allowing consumers to generate their own power and sell excess energy back to the grid.

Global Policies and Investments

Governments worldwide are increasingly supporting renewable energy through legislation, subsidies, and incentives:

- **European Green Deal**: The EU aims to become the world's first climate-neutral continent by 2050. The Green Deal includes investment in renewable energy, energy efficiency, and carbon capture technologies.

- **China's Renewable Energy Push**: China is the world leader in renewable energy capacity, especially in solar and wind energy. Its 14th Five-Year Plan emphasizes continued growth in clean energy, with a goal of reaching carbon neutrality by 2060.

- **U.S. Infrastructure and Climate Plan**: The U.S. is investing heavily in renewable energy through initiatives like the Inflation Reduction Act (IRA), which includes incentives for renewable energy development and energy efficiency projects.

The Future Energy Mix

Renewable energy is expected to account for a larger share of the global energy mix as fossil fuels are gradually phased out. By 2050, renewables could provide over 85% of global electricity, according to IRENA's "World Energy Transitions Outlook." However, achieving this goal will require coordinated global action, technological innovation, and sustained investment in clean energy infrastructure.

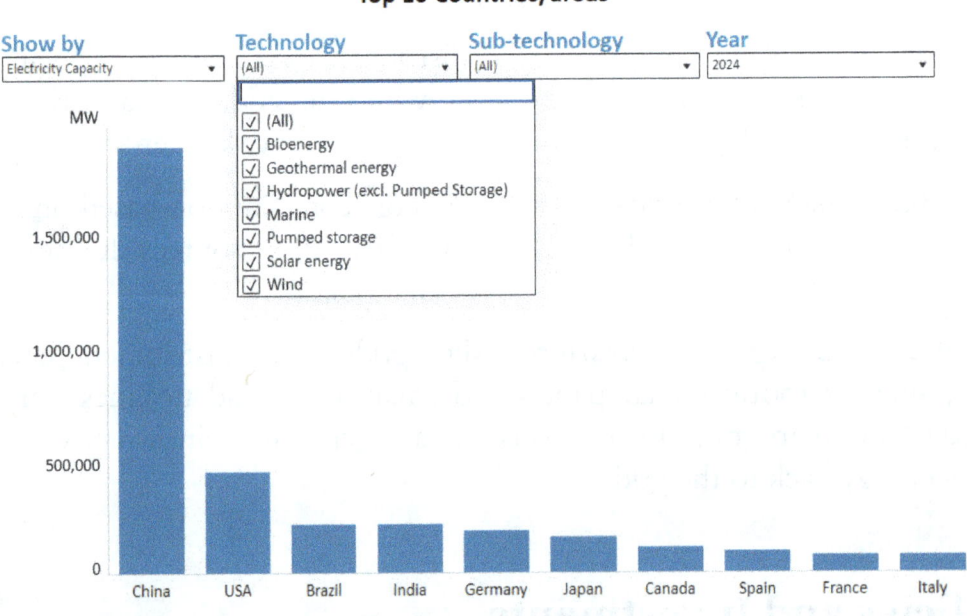

Figure 12.1. Top countries by renewable energy investment and capacity (Country Rankings, 2025)

Policy and Regulation: How Governments Help Promote Renewable Energy

Government policies and regulations are essential for increasing the use of renewable energy sources like solar, wind, and hydropower. These policies help make renewable energy more affordable and accessible, and they encourage businesses and communities to invest in clean energy technologies. Understanding how governments use policies to support renewable energy is important for anyone learning about green energy technologies. These decisions influence the types of energy we use, how clean our environment is, and what our energy future will look like.

What Are Renewable Energy Policies?

Renewable energy policies are rules and guidelines that governments create to support the use of clean energy. These policies can make it easier for companies to build solar farms, wind turbines, and other renewable energy projects. They can also provide financial help to people who want to install solar panels on their homes. Here are some of the ways that policies can encourage renewable energy:

- **Setting Renewable Energy Targets**: Governments set goals for how much of the country's electricity should come from renewable sources by a certain year. For example, the United States has a goal of generating 100% clean electricity by 2035.

- **Offering Financial Incentives**: To make renewable energy more affordable, governments may provide tax credits, grants, or rebates to companies and individuals who invest in renewable technologies. For example, the **Investment Tax Credit (ITC)** in the U.S. allows homeowners and businesses to deduct a percentage of the cost of installing solar panels from their taxes.

Why Do Governments Support Renewable Energy?

Governments support renewable energy for several important reasons:

- **Fight Climate Change**: Renewable energy helps reduce the amount of greenhouse gases released into the atmosphere, which helps combat global warming.

- **Energy Independence**: By using renewable energy sources, countries can reduce their dependence on fossil fuels like coal, oil, and gas, which are often imported from other nations.

- **Job Creation**: The renewable energy industry creates millions of jobs in areas like manufacturing, installation, and maintenance. According to a 2021 report, the renewable energy sector employed more than 12 million people globally, further increased by one million people in the year 2022 as shown in Figure 12.2.

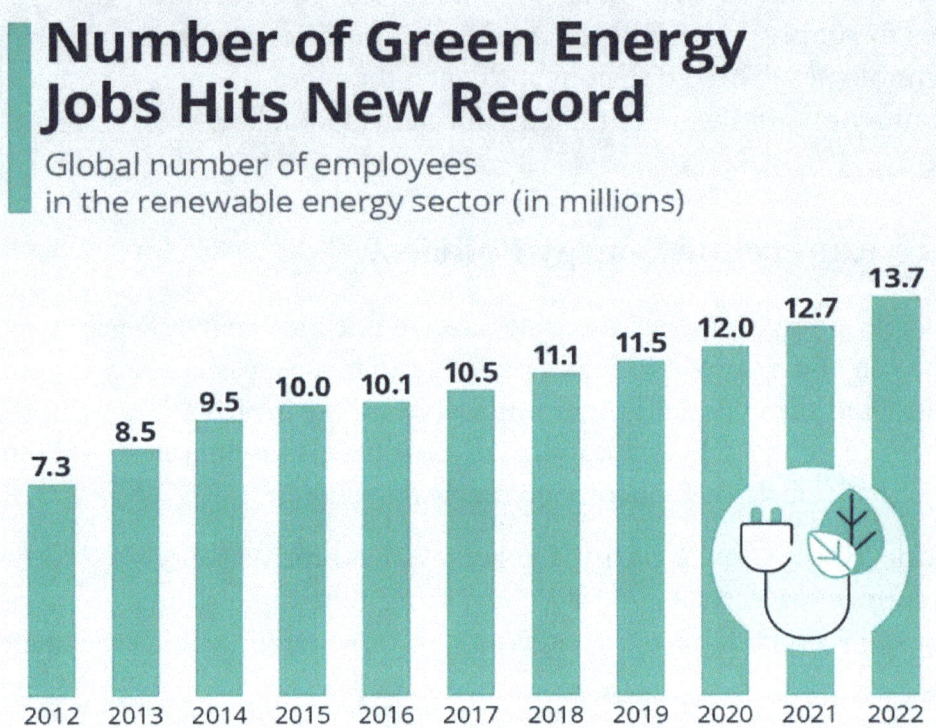

Figure 12.2. Job growth in the renewable energy sector (Fleck, 2023)

Types of Renewable Energy Policies

Governments use a variety of policies to promote renewable energy, each with its own way of supporting clean energy growth.

- **Renewable Portfolio Standards (RPS)**: Some governments require utility companies to generate a certain percentage of their electricity from renewable sources. This policy pushes power companies to invest in wind, solar, and other clean energy technologies. For example, California has a goal of 60% renewable electricity by 2030.

- **Feed-in Tariffs (FiTs)**: In some countries, the government guarantees renewable energy producers (like solar farms or wind turbine operators) a fixed price for the electricity they generate. This provides a stable source of income for renewable energy businesses, encouraging more investment in the sector.

- **Carbon Taxes**: A carbon tax is a fee that companies must pay if they release too much carbon dioxide into the atmosphere. This makes using fossil fuels more expensive and encourages businesses to switch to renewable energy sources, which don't produce carbon emissions as illustrated in Figure 12.3

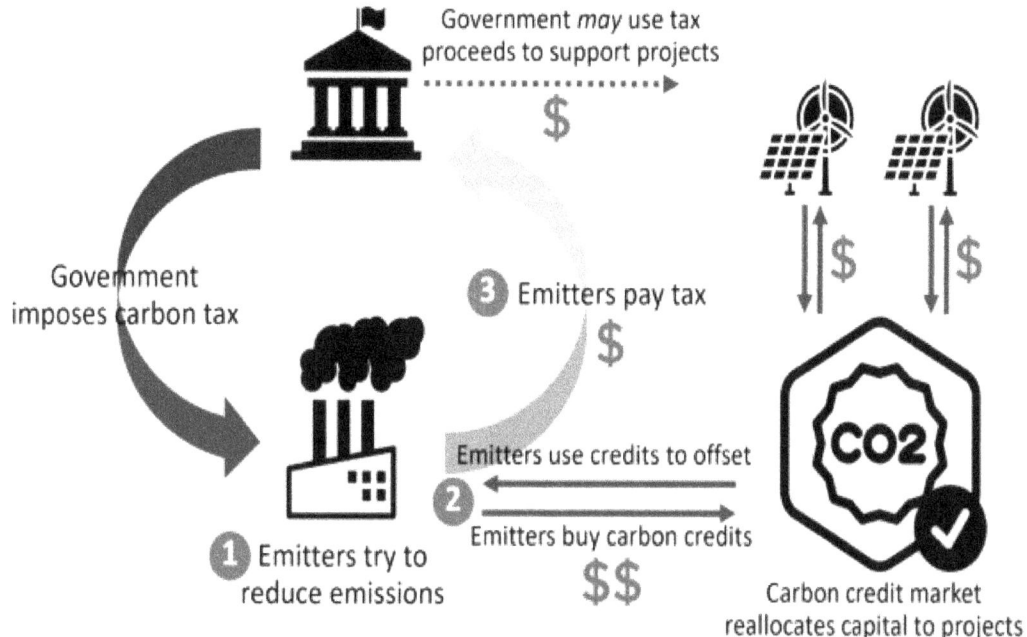

Figure 12.3. Diagram showing how carbon tax works to reduce emissions and encourage renewable energy (Beacon Venture Capital, 2023).

The Role of International Agreements

Policies are not just set by individual countries. In some cases, international agreements also play a major role in advancing renewable energy. One of the most important global agreements is the **Paris Agreement**, where almost every country in the world agreed to work together to limit global warming to below 2°C.

- **Paris Agreement**: This global climate change agreement was signed in 2015. It aims to reduce carbon emissions worldwide, and many countries are using renewable energy policies as part of their plan to meet the goals of this agreement.

Real-World Examples

- **Germany's Energiewende**: Germany is leading the way in renewable energy with its policy known as *Energiewende* (Energy Transition). This policy aims to phase out nuclear and fossil fuels, replacing them with renewables like wind and solar. Germany set a goal to have 80% of its electricity come from renewable sources by 2050.
- **China's Renewable Energy Push**: China is the world's largest producer of renewable energy, especially in solar and wind power. The Chinese government has set strong renewable energy targets and invested heavily in clean energy projects to reduce air pollution and become a global leader in clean technology.

How Policies Help You

If you are interested in a future career in renewable energy, understanding government policies is key. These policies create opportunities for research, innovation, and jobs in renewable energy. They also support the development of new technologies that will make renewable energy even more efficient and widespread in the future.

Did you know? As a student, you could benefit from renewable energy policies too! For example, many universities and colleges offer courses or programs on renewable energy, funded by government grants.

Statistical Insights

The future of renewable energy can be understood better with the following key statistics:

- **Global Renewable Energy Capacity**: As of 2021, global renewable energy capacity reached approximately 3,064 GW, with solar and wind being the most prominent sources. In 2024, global renewable power capacity reached 4,448 GW according to the data provided by IRENA with China leading the World Renewable Energy investment and capacity as shown in Figure 12.1.
- **Job Creation**: The renewable energy sector employed around 12 million people globally in 2020, and this number is expected to grow as more countries expand their renewable energy infrastructure.
- **Renewable Energy Investment**: Global investment in renewable energy exceeded $300 billion in 2021, with the bulk of the investment going to solar and wind projects. Investment in energy storage and green hydrogen is expected to surge in the coming years.

Conclusion

The future of renewable energy holds incredible promise. Through technological advancements, smart policy decisions, and sustainable investment, the world is moving toward a cleaner, more resilient energy future. As young students entering the workforce, you will be part of the generation that drives the renewable energy revolution, solving critical challenges and building a sustainable world for future generations.

Renewable energy is not just the energy of the future; it is the energy of today, rapidly transforming the global landscape as we work together to create a greener planet.

Policies and regulations play a crucial role in making renewable energy a major part of our world's energy system. As you think about your future, it is important to understand how governments are helping to create a cleaner, more sustainable world. Renewable energy isn't just the future of power—it's a key part of creating a healthier planet for all of us.

Chapter 13

Professional Career in Renewable Energy and How to Get Involved

The renewable energy industry is one of the fastest-growing sectors globally, offering diverse career opportunities across engineering, science, policy, and business. For high school and early college students interested in building a rewarding career in renewable energy, there are many paths to explore. This chapter will guide you through what a career in renewable energy looks like, the key skills you will need, the types of jobs available, and how to start preparing for this exciting field.

Why Choose a Career in Renewable Energy?

The world is rapidly transitioning to clean energy to combat climate change and reduce our reliance on fossil fuels. As a result, there is a growing demand for professionals who can help design, implement, and manage renewable energy systems.

- **Job Growth**: The renewable energy sector is expected to create millions of new jobs globally. In 2021 alone, there were over 12 million jobs in the renewable energy industry, and this number continues to rise as more countries invest in solar, wind, hydropower, and other renewable technologies.

- **Positive Impact**: Working in renewable energy allows you to contribute to solving some of the world's biggest challenges, including climate change and energy security. It's a career where you can make a real difference by helping create a more sustainable future.

Career Paths in Renewable Energy

There are a variety of career paths within renewable energy, ranging from technical roles like engineering to business, policy, and communications. Below are some of the most common career options:

- **Engineering**: Energy engineers are professionals who design, analyze, and optimize systems for producing, distributing, and using energy especially in ways that are efficient, cost-effective, and environmentally responsible. Depending on your interest, you could develop expertise and work as:

- o **Solar Energy Engineer**: Designing and installing solar power systems.
- o **Wind Energy Engineer**: Developing wind turbines and optimizing their performance.
- o **Hydropower Engineer**: Working on dams and hydroelectric power stations.
- o **Bioenergy Engineer:** Designing and developing technologies to convert biomass (plant material) into usable energy sources like biofuels (such as bioethanol, biodiesel, and biogas) or electricity.
- o **Battery Engineer**: Developing energy storage systems like lithium-ion batteries.
- **Environmental Scientist**: Studying the environmental impact of renewable energy projects and ensuring that they meet sustainability standards.
- **Energy Analyst**: Evaluating the performance of renewable energy systems, forecasting energy production, and analyzing energy data to make systems more efficient.
- **Policy and Advocacy**: Working in renewable energy policy involves creating and promoting regulations that support the growth of clean energy. Policy specialists often work with governments and environmental organizations to push for clean energy laws.
- **Business and Marketing**: Renewable energy companies need business professionals who can manage projects, develop strategies, and promote renewable technologies to the public. Business roles can include project managers, financial analysts, and marketing specialists.

Key Skills for a Career in Renewable Energy

No matter which path(s) you choose, there are key skills that will help you succeed in the renewable energy industry. Here are some of the most important skills:

- **STEM Knowledge**: A strong foundation in science, technology, engineering, and math (STEM) is essential for many renewable energy jobs. High school students should focus on subjects like physics, chemistry, environmental science, and math to prepare for a career in this field.
- **Problem-Solving**: Renewable energy professionals are constantly finding ways to improve technology and solve energy challenges. Being a good problem-solver is critical for roles like engineering and system design.

- **Communication**: You will need to communicate technical information clearly to non-experts, including policymakers, business executives, and the public. Good Communication skills are also essential if you are working in advocacy or education.
- **Project Management**: Many renewable energy projects, like building a solar farm or wind power station, require careful planning and management. Project management skills help ensure that projects are completed on time and within budget.

How to Get Started in Renewable Energy

Here are the steps you can take to start building a career in renewable energy, whether you are still in high school or starting college:

- **Explore Your Interests**: Start by learning about different types of renewable energy (solar, wind, hydro, biomass, etc.) and think about which area interests you the most. Watching documentaries, reading articles, or attending renewable energy workshops are great ways to explore.
- **Take STEM Classes**: Focus on your STEM education in high school by taking courses in physics, chemistry, biology, and math. Many renewable energy careers require strong analytical and technical skills, which can be developed through these subjects.
- **Participate in Science and Engineering Competitions**: Join science clubs or participate in renewable energy-related science fairs. You can also look for renewable energy challenges or innovation competitions where you can work on projects that apply clean energy concepts.
- **Look for Internships or Volunteer Opportunities**: Gaining hands-on experience is essential. Intern with companies or organizations that are involved in renewable energy. Some internships may be available for high school students, while others are more suited for college students. Volunteering with environmental groups that focus on clean energy can also provide valuable exposure.
- **Pursue Renewable Energy Degrees**: In college, you can major in areas such as environmental science, engineering (chemical, mechanical/industrial, electrical, civil), or energy management. There are also specialized renewable energy programs available at many universities.
- **Get Certifications**: After high school/college, consider getting certifications that

are highly valued in the renewable energy industry. Certifications like the LEED Green Associate, Certified Energy Manager (CEM), and others demonstrate your expertise and commitment to the field.

Career Opportunities for College Graduates

As you move into higher education, opportunities to specialize in renewable energy grow. Some career paths after college include:

- **Renewable Energy Engineer**: Design, test, and oversee the installation of energy systems.

- **Sustainability Consultant**: Advise businesses on how to reduce energy use and integrate renewable technologies.

- **Research Scientist**: Investigate new technologies or improve existing ones in areas like solar cell efficiency or advanced battery storage.

- **Energy Auditor**: Analyze a building's energy use and suggest ways to make it more efficient.

Figure 13.1. Career pathways in renewable energy from high school through professional certifications.

The Role of Internships and Networking

Internships and networking are crucial for getting started in the renewable energy sector. They allow you to gain real-world experience, build professional relationships, and better understand what it is like to work in the field.

- **Internships**: Seek out internships at renewable energy companies, government agencies, or nonprofit organizations. These internships will help you gain practical experience and make valuable connections.

- **Networking**: Attend renewable energy conferences, webinars, and job fairs. Networking with professionals in the industry can open doors to job opportunities and mentorship.

Statistics and Growth Potential

- The renewable energy sector is projected to grow by 50% over the next decade, creating thousands of new jobs across the U.S. and globally.

- Solar power has seen a 167% increase in job growth over the past 10 years, making it one of the fastest growing sectors in renewable energy. As shown in Figure 13.2, the renewable energy sector is experiencing substantial growth, creating a demand for various skilled professionals to support the transition to a cleaner energy economy.

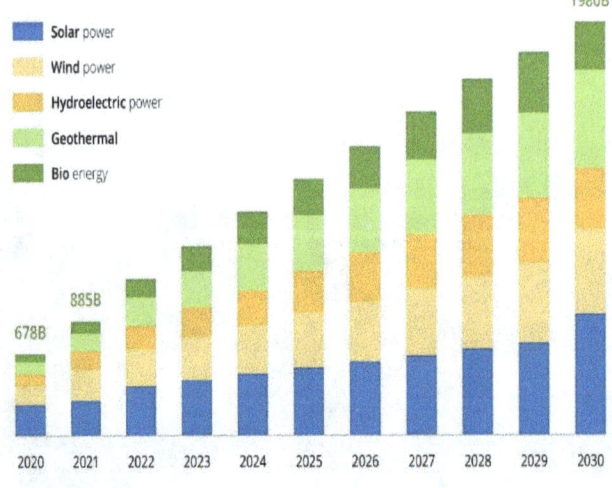

Figure 13.2. Types of renewable energy jobs and their expected growth from 2020 to 2030 (Suri, 2024)

Getting Involved via Community Initiatives and Personal Actions

In addition to pursuing formal education and careers in renewable energy, high school and college students can start making a difference through community initiatives and personal actions. The following activities not only build your knowledge and experience, but also help raise awareness about the importance of renewable energy and sustainable living:

1. Join or Start a Renewable Energy Club

Many high schools and colleges have clubs or organizations focused on environmental sustainability and renewable energy. Joining one of these groups is a great way to connect with like-minded individuals, learn more about renewable energy, and work on projects that make a real difference.

- **What You Can Do**: Help organize events like energy-saving campaigns, lead educational workshops on renewable energy, or participate in local clean energy initiatives.
- **Starting a Club**: If your school doesn't have a renewable energy or sustainability club, you could consider starting one. Your club could focus on solar panel installations, recycling programs, or even a community garden powered by clean energy. This will not only help your school reduce its carbon footprint but also teach fellow students about renewable energy.

2. Volunteer with Local Environmental Organizations

There are many local environmental organizations and nonprofits that focus on promoting renewable energy and sustainability. Volunteering with these groups can provide hands-on experience in areas like installing solar panels, organizing clean energy advocacy events, or even conducting energy audits.

- **Examples of Actions**: Participate in tree-planting drives, help with community energy-saving projects, or assist in building small renewable energy installations, like solar-powered charging stations in public parks.
- **Benefits**: Volunteering can build your resume, expand your network, and provide real- world experience that will be valuable when you start applying for jobs in the renewable energy industry.

3. Participate in Local Renewable Energy Programs

Some cities and states offer programs that allow residents to support or even use renewable energy directly. For example, many local governments have community solar programs where you can subscribe to a portion of a solar farm's energy and receive credit on your utility bill.

- **What You Can Do**: Encourage your family or school to participate in a community solar program or opt for a clean energy plan from your local utility provider if available.

4. Personal Actions for Renewable Energy

Taking personal action is one of the easiest ways to get involved with renewable energy, and it helps reduce your own carbon footprint. Here are some steps you can take today:

- **Reduce Energy Consumption**: The first step toward supporting renewable energy is using less energy overall. Simple actions like turning off lights, using energy-efficient appliances, and unplugging devices when not in use can make a big difference.

- **Install Renewable Energy Systems at Home**: If your family is interested, consider installing solar panels or small-scale wind turbines at your home. While the initial investment may be higher, renewable energy systems can reduce your household's reliance on fossil fuels and lower utility bills in the long run. Many governments offer financial incentives like tax credits to offset the costs of these installations.

- **Choose Energy-Efficient Transportation**: Opt for biking, walking, or public transportation instead of driving. If you or your family are looking for a new car, consider purchasing an electric vehicle (EV), which can run on renewable energy if charged using solar or wind power.

5. Advocate for Clean Energy in Your Community

One of the most powerful ways to get involved in renewable energy is by advocating for policies and programs that support clean energy at the local, state, or national level.

- **How to Advocate**: You can write to your local representatives, participate in public hearings, or join clean energy campaigns that push for renewable energy projects and policies in your community. Use social media platforms to spread awareness about the benefits of renewable energy and encourage others to get involved.

6. Internships and Fellowships Focused on Community Renewable Energy

Some organizations offer internships or fellowships focused on renewable energy policy, community outreach, and environmental education. These opportunities allow you to work on real projects that promote renewable energy, help develop clean energy policies or educate the public about sustainable energy.

- **Examples**: Intern with a renewable energy advocacy group, participate in a solar panel installation project, or help run educational programs that teach others about renewable energy.

Conclusion

A career in renewable energy offers exciting opportunities to make a positive impact on the environment, while working in a field with significant job growth. By focusing on your STEM education, gaining hands-on experience, and staying informed about the latest clean energy developments, you can prepare for a rewarding career that helps shape the future of our planet. Whether you want to be an engineer, a scientist, or a policy expert, the renewable energy sector needs passionate, skilled individuals to lead the way. Whether you join a club, volunteer, or make personal lifestyle changes, there are many ways to get involved in renewable energy while still in school. These actions help you gain valuable experience, make a positive impact on the environment, and prepare you for a future career in this exciting and rapidly growing field. Small actions can lead to big changes, especially when many people work together toward a cleaner, more sustainable energy future.

Chapter 14

Essential Equations for Renewable Energy Calculations

Understanding how to calculate power output, energy generation, and efficiency is crucial in renewable energy systems. The following basic equations help students, engineers, and technicians analyze and compare technologies like solar panels, wind turbines, hydropower systems, and more.

1. Solar Energy

Power from Solar Panel:
$$P = A \times G \times \eta$$

Where:
- P = Power output (W)
- A = Area of the solar panel (m²)
- G = Solar irradiance (W/m²)
- η = Efficiency of the solar panel (usually 15% - 22%)

Energy from Solar Panel Over Time:
$$E = P \times t$$

Where:
- E = Energy (Wh or kWh)
- t = Time (hours)

2. Wind Energy

Power in the Wind (obtained from kinetic energy in relation to time):
$$P = \tfrac{1}{2} \times \rho \times A \times v^3$$

Where:
- ρ = Air density (~1.225 kg/m³) depending on Air Temperature
- A = Swept area (m²)
- v = Wind speed (m/s)

Actual Power Output:

$$P_{actual} = \tfrac{1}{2} \times \rho \times A \times v^3 \times C_p \times \eta$$

Where:

- C_p = Power coefficient

Theoretical maximum wind power is defined by the Betz Limit as ~0.59 (i.e., at most, a turbine can extract about 59% of the incoming kinetic energy); realistic ~0.35–0.45.

3. Hydropower

Hydropower Potential:

$$P = \eta \times \rho \times g \times Q \times H$$

Where:
- η = Efficiency of the system
- ρ = Water density (1000 kg/m³)
- g = Gravitational Acceleration (9.81 m/s²)
- Q = Flow rate (m³/s)
- H = Effective Head (m)

4. Biomass Energy

Energy in biomass fuel:

$$E = m \times HHV$$

Where:

E = Energy released (kJ or MJ)

m = Mass of biomass (kg)

HHV = Higher Heating Value (kJ/kg), varies by feedstock

Gasification/Pyrolysis Efficiency:

$$\eta = (\text{Useful Output} / \text{Input Energy}) \times 100\%$$

5. Geothermal Energy

Thermal Power Output:

$$P = \dot{m} \times C_p \times \Delta T$$

Where:

$\dot{m}$ = Mass flow rate of fluid (kg/s)

Cp = Specific heat capacity (~4.18 kJ/kg·K for water)

ΔT = Temperature change (°C or K)

6. Tidal Energy

Tidal Power:

$$P = \tfrac{1}{2} \times \rho \times A \times v^3$$

Same formula as wind energy, since tides and waves are moving fluids

Water density ρ is ~1000 kg/m³, making power much higher than wind for same speeds (v)

7. Energy Storage (Batteries)

Stored Energy in Battery:

$$E = V \times I \times t$$

Where:

E = Energy (Wh or kWh)

V = Voltage (V)

I = Current (A)

t = Time (h)

Round-trip Efficiency:

$$\eta = (E\_output / E\_input) \times 100\%$$

Typical lithium-ion batteries have 85%–95% round-trip efficiency.

8. General Efficiency Equation

This expresses how well a system converts input energy into useful output.

$$\eta = (\text{Useful Output} / \text{Input Energy}) \times 100\%$$

9. Capacity Factor Equation

The capacity factor tells us how much electricity a renewable energy system actually produces over a period, compared to how much it could have produced if it ran at full power the whole time.

Capacity Factor:

CF= [Energy generated (Actual Energy Output) / Energy Capacity (Maximum Possible Energy Output over Same Time)] × 100%

$$CF = E\_actual/E\_rated * 100\%$$

Where:

E_actual = Actual energy produced (kWh)

E_rated = Rated or maximum capacity (kW)

t = Time period (hours)

The above equations are summarized in Figure 14.1.

Energy Source	Key Equation	Efficiency Range	Typical Capacity Factor	Notes
Solar	$P = A \cdot G \cdot \eta$	15% – 22%	15% – 25%	Depends on sunlight hours and panel tilt
Wind	$P = \frac{1}{2}\rho A v^3$	35% – 45%	25% – 45%	Highly sensitive to wind speed and location
Hydropower	$P = \eta \cdot \rho \cdot g \cdot Q \cdot H$	80% – 95%	40% – 60%	High reliability in regions with consistent flow
Biomass	$E = m \cdot HHV$	20% – 35% (thermal)	60% – 85%	Available year-round; dispatchable energy source
Geothermal	$P = \dot{m} \cdot C_p \cdot \Delta T$	10% – 20% (electric), up to 90% (direct use)	70% – 90%	Stable and continuous source of energy
Tidal	$P = \frac{1}{2}\rho A v^3$	80% – 90% (mechanical)	30% – 60%	Predictable, but site-specific
Battery Storage	$E = V \cdot I \cdot t$	85% – 95% (round-trip)	N/A	Not a source, but stores and delivers energy

Figure 14.1. Summary of key equations for estimating power output

Chapter 15

Resources and Further Reading

Books and Articles

- Aghmadi, A., & Mohammed, O. A. (2024). Energy storage systems: technologies and high-power applications. *Batteries*, *10*(4), 141.

- Alamu, S. O., Wemida, A., Tsegaye, T., & Oguntimein, G. (2021). Sustainability assessment of municipal solid waste in Baltimore USA. *Sustainability*, *13*(4), 1915.

- Alamu, S. O., Caballes, M. J. L., Qian X, Lee S., & Hunter Jr, J. G. (2021). Efficient Biomass Conversion Process to Sustainable Energy. *Journal of Construction Project Management and Innovation*, *11*(1), 180-190.

- Boyle, G. (2024). Renewable Energy: Power For a Sustainable Future. TIDEE: TERI Information Digest on Energy and Environment, 23(1/2), 120-120.

- Boyle, G. (2012). Renewable Energy: Power for a Sustainable Future. Oxford University Press.

- Duffie, J. A., & Beckman, W. A. (2013). Solar Engineering of Thermal Processes. Wiley.

- Faaij, A. (2006). Modern biomass conversion technologies. *Mitigation and adaptation strategies for global change*, *11*(2), 343-375.

- Kaltschmitt, M., Streicher, W., & Wiese, A. (Eds.). (2007). Renewable energy: technology, economics and environment. Springer Science & Business Media.

- Kemp, W. H. (2005). The renewable energy handbook: a guide to rural independence, off-grid and sustainable living.

- Osman, A. I., Mehta, N., Elgarahy, A. M., Hefny, M., Al-Hinai, A., Al-Muhtaseb, A. A. H., & Rooney, D. W. (2022). Hydrogen production, storage, utilisation and environmental impacts: a review. *Environmental Chemistry Letters*, *20*(1), 153-188.

- Panwar, N. L., Kaushik, S. C., & Kothari, S. (2011). Role of renewable energy sources in environmental protection: A review. *Renewable and sustainable energy reviews*, *15*(3), 1513-1524.

- Randolph, J., & Masters, G. M. (2008). *Energy for sustainability: Technology, planning, policy.* Island Press.

- Tester, J. W., Drake, E. M., Driscoll, M. J., Golay, M. W., & Peters, W. A.

(2012). *Sustainable energy: choosing among options*. MIT press.

Websites and Organizations

- U.S. DOE Office of Energy Efficiency & Renewable Energy. https://www.energy.gov/eere
- Global renewables outlook: Energy transformation 2050. IRENA. (2020, April 1). https://www.irena.org/publications/2020/Apr/Global-Renewables-Outlook-2020
- U.S. Energy Information Administration - EIA - independent statistics and analysis. Waste-to-energy (MSW) in depth - U.S. Energy Information Administration (EIA). (n.d.). https://www.eia.gov/energyexplained/biomass/waste-to-energy-in-depth.php
- Palma, T. D. (2024, December 20). *Types of PV panels - what are the differences*. BibLus. https://biblus.accasoftware.com/en/types-of-pv-panels-what-are-the-differences/
- IEA (2023). Renewables 2023: Analysis and Forecast to 2028. https://www.iea.org/reports/renewables-2023
- Statista. (2025, April 30). Global cumulative installed capacity of wind power 2024, by country. https://www.statista.com/statistics/217522/cumulative-installed-capacity-of-wind-power-worldwide/
- Sonika, S. (2023, September 5). *Fermentation: Definition, process and types of fermentation*. Career Power School. https://www.careerpower.in/school/biology/fermentation
- Cambi Group AS. (2025, January 29). *Biogas from wastewater: A sustainable energy solution*. Cambi. https://www.cambi.com/blog/biogas-wastewater
- The Business Research Company. (2025). Biomass Electricity Global Market Report 2025. In *The Business Research Company*. https://www.thebusinessresearchcompany.com/report/biomass-electricity-global-market-report
- Zoting, S. (2025, May 28). *Lithium-ion Battery Market Size to Worth USD 499.31 Billion by 2034*. https://www.precedenceresearch.com/lithium-ion-battery-market
- Park, J. (2024, December 9). COP29: Can the world reach 1.5TW of energy

- storage by 2030?. Power Technology. https://www.power-technology.com/features/cop29-can-the-world-reach-1-5tw-of-energy-storage-by-2030/?cf-view
- Fleck, A. (2023, November 13). Number of Green Energy Jobs Hits New Record. *Statista Daily Data.* https://www.statista.com/chart/31242/employees-in-the-renewable-energy-sector/
- Beacon Venture Capital. (2023, February 28). *Carbon Post Tax Economy.* https://www.beaconvc.fund/knowledge/carbon-post-tax-economy
- U.S. Energy Information Administration - EIA - independent statistics and analysis. Delivery to consumers - U.S. Energy Information Administration (EIA). (n.d.). https://www.eia.gov/energyexplained/electricity/delivery-to-consumers.php
- Country Rankings. (2005). https://www.irena.org/Data/View-data-by-topic/Capacity-and-Generation/Country-Rankings
- Gevme. (2023, August 2). *The 3 pillars of Sustainability.* https://www.gevme.com/en/blog/the-three-pillars-of-sustainability/
- Suri, R. (2024, July 24). Blog. *Luxoft.* https://www.luxoft.com/blog/renewable-energy-types-opportunities-disadvantages
- Wolf, S. (2025, January 28). Bifacial Solar Panels: What Are They & How Do They Work? *Paradise Energy Solutions.* https://www.paradisesolarenergy.com/blog/what-are-bifacial-solar-panels
- Kennedy, R. (2022, September 16). *Nearly one in ten K-12 schools have adopted Solar Energy.* pv magazine USA. https://pv-magazine-usa.com/2022/09/16/nearly-one-in-ten-k-12-schools-in-the-u-s-have-adopted-solar-energy/
- Schools make the grade for clean energy in the U.S. - U.S. energy foundation. (n.d.). https://www.ef.org/2023/08/23/schools-make-the-grade-for-clean-energy-in-the-u-s/
- How do fish survive hydropower dams?. Energy.gov. (2024, April 29). https://www.energy.gov/eere/water/articles/how-do-fish-survive-hydropower-dams
- Tamara Birch. (2025, March 13). The Pros and cons of renewable energy. The Eco Experts. https://www.theecoexperts.co.uk/news/pros-and-cons-of-renewable-energy

- RBioEnergy. My blog. (2024). https://rbioenergy.com/

Glossary

Algal/Algae: Microscopic or larger plant-like organisms that grow in water and can be used to produce biofuels.

Alternating Current (AC): A type of electric current that reverses direction periodically, used in most power transmission systems.

Anaerobic: A process that takes place without oxygen, such as anaerobic digestion to make biogas.

Biochemical: Energy conversion processes that use biological systems, such as fermentation or digestion by microbes.

Bifacial Solar Panel: A solar panel that can capture sunlight on both its front and back surfaces, producing more electricity than traditional one-sided panels.

Biofuel: A type of fuel made from renewable biological materials such as plants, waste, or algae.

Biomass: Organic material that comes from plants and animals and can be used as a renewable energy source.

Biorefinery: A facility that converts biomass (plants, waste, or algae) into fuels, electricity, or other valuable products, similar to how a petroleum refinery works.

Carbon Footprint: The total amount of greenhouse gases (especially carbon dioxide) emitted by human activities.

Circuit: A closed loop through which electricity flows.

Climate Change: Long-term changes in global temperature and weather patterns, often caused by human activities like burning fossil fuels.

Decarbonization: The process of reducing carbon dioxide (CO_2) emissions from energy systems to fight climate change.

Distillation: The process of heating a liquid mixture to separate its components based on different boiling points, often used in biofuel production.

Distribution Lines: Power lines that deliver electricity from substations to homes and businesses.

Energy Efficiency: Using less energy to perform the same task or achieve the same outcome.

Environmental Impact: The effect an energy technology or project has on the natural environment, including air, water, land, and living things.

Esterification: A chemical reaction used to produce biodiesel by reacting fats or oils with alcohol.

Feedstock: The raw material (such as crops, waste, or algae) used to produce energy or fuels.

Fossil Fuels: Non-renewable energy sources like coal, oil, and natural gas formed from ancient plant and animal remains.

Generator: A device that converts mechanical energy into electrical energy.

Grid: The network that delivers electricity from power plants to users.

Hydroelectric: Electricity produced by moving water, usually from rivers or dams.

Hydrolysis: A chemical process that uses water to break down larger molecules into smaller ones, important in converting biomass into sugars.

Hydropower: Energy from moving water, usually produced by dams.

Innovation: The process of creating new ideas, products, or methods that improve existing technologies.

Kilowatt-hour (kWh): A unit of energy used to measure electricity usage.

kWp (solar): Stands for "kilowatt-peak," the maximum power output a solar panel can produce under ideal sunlight conditions.

Liquefaction: The process of turning gas into liquid, often used for easier storage or transport of fuels.

LCOE (Levelized Cost of Energy): A measure of the average cost of producing electricity from a power plant over its lifetime, including construction, operation, and maintenance, divided by the total electricity generated. It helps compare the true cost of different energy sources.

Methanol: A simple alcohol that can be used as fuel or as a building block for making biofuels.

Microorganisms: Tiny living organisms, such as bacteria or fungi, that can help break down biomass into useful energy products.

Onshore: Refers to wind farms or energy facilities located on land.

Offshore: Refers to wind farms or energy facilities built in bodies of water, usually at sea.

Photovoltaic (PV) Cell: A device that converts sunlight directly into electricity.

Policy: Government rules, laws, or guidelines that shape how energy is produced, used, and regulated.

Renewable Energy: Energy that comes from natural sources that are constantly replenished, like solar or wind.

Scalability: The ability of a technology or system to expand in size or capacity without losing efficiency.

Smart Grids: Advanced electricity networks that use digital technology to monitor, manage, and deliver energy more efficiently.

Solar Panel: A device that captures sunlight and converts it into electricity.

Stream Energy: Power generated from the constant movement of water in rivers or streams.

Sustainability: Meeting current needs without compromising the ability of future generations to meet theirs.

Thermochemical: Energy conversion processes that use heat and chemical reactions, such as combustion, gasification or pyrolysis.

Tidal: Energy harnessed from the natural rise and fall of ocean tides to generate electricity.

Transformer: An electrical device that changes (steps up or steps down) voltage so electricity can travel efficiently through power lines.

Transmission Lines: High-voltage wires that carry electricity long distances from power plants to substations.

Turbine: A machine with blades that spin when driven by wind, water, steam, or gas to generate electricity.

Wake (wind turbine): The disturbed air flow created behind a wind turbine that can reduce the efficiency of nearby turbines.

Wind Turbine: A machine that uses wind energy to spin blades connected to a generator.

This book offers an engaging and easy-to-understand introduction to renewable energy for students at all levels—from high school to college, and anyone just beginning to explore sustainable technologies. With clear explanations and relatable examples, it breaks down complex ideas and encourages readers to think critically about the role of clean energy in shaping our world. It's designed not just to inform, but to inspire future innovators, engineers, and everyday change makers.

Another Book by the Author

Renewable Energy: The Fuel of the Future

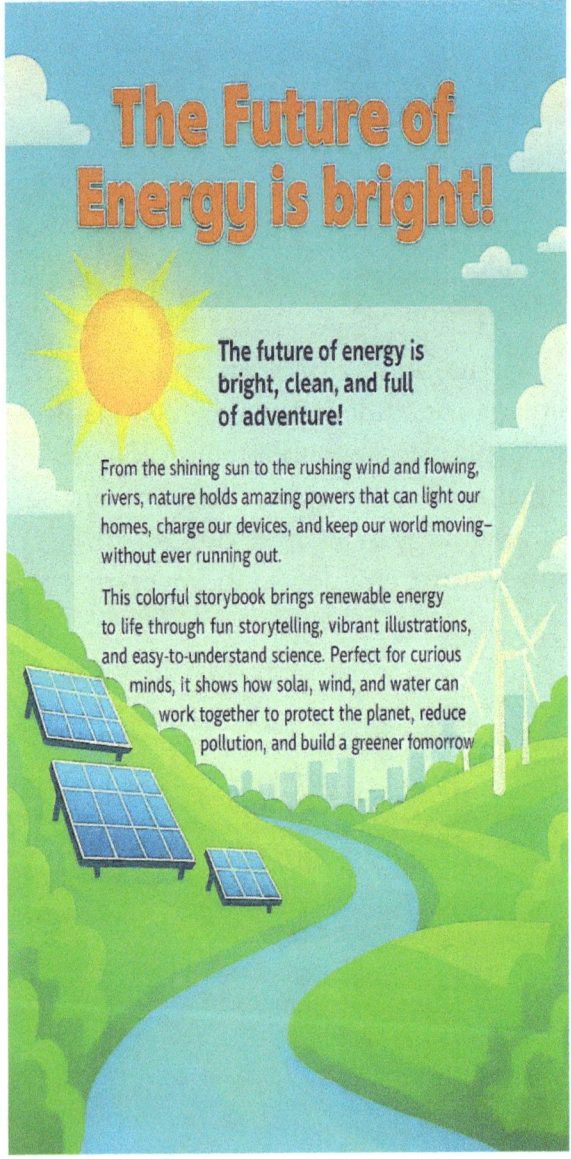

www.ingramcontent.com/pod-product-compliance
Lightning Source LLC
Chambersburg PA
CBHW081210170426
43198CB00018B/2912